ICE CARVING

by HIDEO HASEGAWA

English Language Translation by NORMAN BRASLOW

Norman Braslow received his B.A. and M.A. degrees in History at Pacific Union College and subsequently studied Japanese at the Monterey Institute of Foreign Studies under Professor Jun Mink. He is presently employed at Toyota Motor Sales, U.S.A., as Administration Assistant to the President.
Norman Braslow will receive his Phd in Japanese History at the University of Southern California Los Angeles, California.

EDITED BY: Jackie Athey

First Edition/First Printing

Continental Publications
PALOS VERDES, CA. 90274

HASEGAWA HIDEO

Born in Tokyo 1925. After graduating from high school, joined the Navy Air Corps. After demobilization, studied cooking in various places. In 1961 was a cook in the New Japan Hotel, where he is at present. He is also consultant to the Japanese Culinary Association as a European-style lecturer, thereby guiding the younger men. He participated in the 5th Cooking Olympics, winning first place for his ice carving, which acknowledges his brilliant work.

(Note: The above way of writing the author's name is the traditional Japanese style, with the family name first and the given name last.)

Copyright 1974; Japanese and International Editions by: Hideo Hasegawa

Published in Japanese Edition, December 5, 1974 by: Shibata Shoten Publishing Co.
3-33-5 Hongo, Bunkyo-ku
Tokyo 109 Japan

Copyright 1978; English Language Editions by: Continental Publications

First Edition in English Language: 5,000
International Standard Book Number: 0-916096-11-4
Library of Congress Catalog Card Number: 77-083288
Manufactured in the United States of America

Acknowledgements: Jacket Design by Paul Coconis; Typography by Phyllis MacFadden; Graphic layout and production by S. Hayashi and Barbara Hoffman; Color Separations by Vivi Colour, Covina, California; Half-tones and stripping by Grafics West, Burbank, California; Cover printed by Clark Lithograph, Los Angeles, California; Book printed by Penn Litho Graphics, Whittier, California; Edition binding by SEBCO, Monterey Park, California; Coordinator, Roto-Litho, Inc., Los Angeles, California.

Continental Publications
PALOS VERDES, CALIFORNIA 90274

A-1 MIKOSHI (A portable Shrine for processions)
This was made for a reception in a hotel. It was made of twelve separate pieces of ice and took four hours to make, without using a freezer.

A-2 FALCONS
These falcons were carefully designed to make sure that they balance each other. It was made from nine pieces of ice and took three hours to build.

A-3 KOTOBUKI ("Congratulations")
This was made for a dish of smoked salmon.

A-4 MIYAJIMA NO TORII
This is a famous shrine in Japan.

A-5 DRAGON
This was made for a reception. It was made from eight pieces of ice and took eight hours to carve.

A-6 Mythical Chinese Lions and a "Magic Hammer."

A-7 ANGEL and PHOENIXES
This was made for a company party.

RECOMMENDATION

In the history of Japanese cooking, French cooking was introduced fairly recently to Japan, but as it has spread throughout the country, the state of the art has improved so that it is now quite remarkable.

Ice carving was developed by the French to enhance their foods with a feeling of refreshment and beauty. When French cuisine was introduced to Japan, ice carving came with it. Now, Japanese ice carving seems to be the finest in the world, due I think, to our skillful and artistic nature.

I think for basic knowledge and skills, Hideo Hasegawa's book on Ice Carving is one of the best the industry has to offer.

I am sure that the publication of this book on ice carving will give young cooks encouragement in the special art of Ice Carving which is respected all over the world as well as in Japan.

Monjiro Saito
Dean, Japanese Culinary Association

PREFACE

I have been drawing and carving since I was a child. Sometimes when I was in the midst of it I would forget to eat. I had thought of becoming an artist, but the war broke out, and I had to work in war-related industry like everyone else. I worked in a machine shop for two years and then applied to the Navy. When the war ended, I was in a Philippine prisoner-of-war camp, where I organized an art group under the guidance of the oil-painter Hiroshi Shihara.

I had been drawing and sculpting with this group before I returned to Japan in 1945. After my return, I had hoped to study under the master sumi-painter Hishigawa. But times were hard, and I became an apprentice in a restaurant learning to cook; today I still work as a cook. Yet, even during that time I occasionally worked as a billboard painter, because I just could not give up painting altogether.

The first time I saw ice carving was at a buffet party at an American occupation forces camp in 1947. I thought I had never seen such a beautiful party in my life; the food was displayed beautifully, and the lighting was used effectively, but it was the ice carving that made a very strong impression on me. It was after that party that I became truly interested in cooking, yet it was not until Christmas, in 1957, that I finally started ice carving. I used only a carpenter's chisel and just "carved my own way." Today, I do not even remember what I first carved, but I was sure then that I could make something. I did not start ice carving as a career until the opening at the New Japan Hotel in Akasaka, Tokyo, in 1960. Since then, I have made many ice carvings. When I have finished, I always see minor blemishes and room for improvement in them. I am always aware of how many physical conditions affect my work. I feel the only way to achieve any progress in my skill is to keep practicing as much as possible. I hope someday to accomplish real works of art. I also hope that this book will help you develop skill in ice carving, by guiding you from the beginning pictures to the difficult combination sculptures. I hope you will refer to this book often while learning the art of ice carving.

Hideo Hasegawa

CONTENTS

CONTENTS

All work performed in this book at
Hotel New Japan, Tokyo, Japan and
Grand Hotel, Hiroshima, Japan.
Photography - Shinubu Ari   Koji Hayashi

1 氷彫刻の基礎

THE BASICS OF ICE CARVING

1 氷彫刻について

INTRODUCTION TO ICE CARVING

Ice carvings are made in many different sizes, from single pieces of 10 Kg. (22 lbs.) each. In northern Japan, huge carvings are made from the permanent ice layer. Recently, ice carving has come to be used in hotels, restaurants, and even coffee shops throughout Japan. The carvings are usually used in receptions, formal dinners, and wedding parties, where they create a mood of beauty and elegance. They are most frequently used with food, but they also have commercial advertising uses. Ice carvings are used the year around, but are more popular in the summer because they give a cool, refreshing feeling. In northern Japan in the winter, huge commercial carvings are made from the permanent ice during the winter festivals. Ice carving came to Japan from France with Master Akiyama around 1917 or 1918. However, it did not become popular until about 1955. Since then, however, it is becoming more popular every year.

When I first participated in the 1970 cooking Olympics in San Francisco, I exhibited my ice carving. However, it was very difficult and expensive to obtain ice because the ice was made to order under contract with the hotel or restaurant. I found quite a difference between how the ice is made in Japan and how it is made in America. Using stone carver's tools and working in freezers at 5° C, took as much as four days to finish a piece. Also, the size of the American ice was a little larger than the standard Japanese sizes of 135 Kg, although it was free of air bubbles.

I have not seen ice carving in any other American or European cities, but from what I saw in San Francisco, it appears to me that the basic composition and the use of the tools of the Japanese are better than any others. Perhaps, this is because we have much more opportunity to practice as ice is so readily available in Japan.

Before starting to carve, please pay attention to the following preliminary matters: ice selection, basic outline, tools, proper procedures, and how the finished piece should look. After you have taken care of these matters, you may start carving, proceeding step by step, from beginner pieces, through intermediate pieces, to advanced pieces.

2. HOW TO SELECT ICE

There is no special ice for ice carving, so you must purchase ice from a regular ice dealer. However, the ice cannot have large air bubbles nor can it be too brittle.

(1) Size of Ice.

In Japan, ice is sold in a standard size of 56 cm wide, 100 cm long, and 27 cm deep. The weight is 135 Kg. The ice is made from normal drinking water.

In North America, ice is sold in a standard size of 20" wide, 42" long, and 10" deep. The weight is 300 pounds.

(2) Quality of Ice.

As stated previously, the ice should be as free as possible from air bubbles and should be as strong and clear as possible.

(3) Ice for Carving.

Since the ice is a standard size in Japan, when you want to make small carvings, you must cut the block of ice down to the proper size. Blocks of ice are cut in one-half cuts, one-third cuts, one-fourth cuts, one-sixth cuts and one-twelfth cuts (see pp. 10-11).

- Be sure of the quality of the ice.
- The important thing about the quality of the ice is its condition. The quality of the ice determines the longevity of the piece one carves. If the ice is in a freezer too long, it becomes hard and very fragile due to the changing temperatures. Of course, ice which is out of a freezer too long becomes watery and very fragile. The best ice is that which has been kept in a freezer at 5° C (23°F) for about only one day since it was made. This is the kind of ice that you should use.
- Do not use fragile ice. When making the standard cuts from the block of ice, a gasoline powered machine saw should be used as beginners find it difficult to cut properly with a hand saw.

3. HOW TO PLAN AN ICE CARVING

When you plan an ice carving, you must be sure that it will be balanced.

- When you plan your carving, you must take the dimensions of your ice into account. For example, the shape of a cube or sphere can only be as wide as your block of ice and cannot be the size of your surface dimensions.
- Since ice comes in a standard size, you must be aware of these limiting dimensions when you plan your carving. Hence, the size of your carving must be determined by the size of the ice blocks, and not by the size of the carving which you envision.
- If you try to use the full size of your ice block, your carving will usually come out flat and two-dimensional.
- An emphasis must be put on the subject of the carving rather than its stand. When you plan such figures as a fish on a wave or a fish in seaweed, there must be more emphasis on the fish than on the seaweed or wave.
- When you compose animals, it is best to express the animal in motion. The figure of a fish is more two-dimensional than other animals, so you will find its geometric form easy to make, and its motion easy to represent.
- When planning your figure, you cannot forget that your figure has to be on a stand, and that this stand must be able to support the animal or fish. For example, if your carving is a fish, a rock or waves would serve as a suitable stand. Such a figure would be good to use as either a small carving or a huge sculpture. However, when you plan a large size carving made of combined blocks of ice, you must be even more careful to make sure that your piece will remain in balance. Also, you will have to pay more attention to the emphasis of your subject by its place in the carving and by the composition.

Combination carving is usually used in parties and receptions. Because of this, ice carving is becoming one of the main items used to give a good atmosphere to an occasion. The sponsor sometimes will request a carving that involves a standard subject or sometimes will want you to compose the carving according to their needs. You must be careful to emphasize the purpose of the sponsor; however, if you do not have specific instructions, you can choose the emphasis of your carving from the purpose of the party.

4. HOW TO COMPOSE THE BASIC OUTLINE

Once you have chosen the subject of your carving, you must make the outline on the block of ice. First, etch the outline with a flat chisel. After you have drawn the outline with an angle chisel. Do not use the angle chisel first, because if a mistake is made, the deeper lines will melt.

5. TOOLS

The necessary tools are:

HAND SAW

There are many kinds of hand saws.

- The large-size hand saw is sold at the ice dealers in Japan.
  This useful tool is 450 mm long and is made of thick steel.
- The medium-size hand saw is 390 mm long, and its blade is a little thicker than that of the large-size hand saw. You can cut a large piece of ice with this saw, but the blade bends too easily. It is best used on middle-sized pieces that are of a size that one person can carry.

- The small-size hand saw is 300 cm long, and it is made especially for ice carving. It is very useful for small carvings, and should be considered essential.
- The pistol-shaped hand saw is one-third the length of the small-size hand saw. Its tip is pointed. This useful saw is used to make small cuts in the ice.

FLAT CHISELS

There are many kinds of chisels:long, short, side, narrow, thick, and thin. It is best to use the thick-bladed chisels.

- The small flat chisel has a width of 40 mm, a blade length of 80 mm, and a handle of 150 mm. The blade should be thick. This is a very useful tool, and you should have two of them.
- The medium-sized flat chisel has a width 50 mm, a blade length of 150 mm, and a handle of 330 mm. Although there are many sizes between this medium size and the small size, these two have the correct dimensions for carving. They are also used for the larger carvings.
- The very small flat chisel has a width of 24 mm, a blade length of 170 mm, and a handle of 160 mm. This long chisel is used to dig into small deep places. One of these is needed.

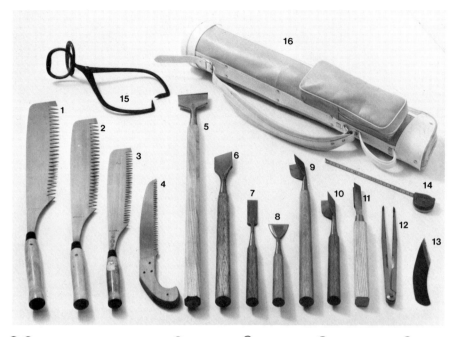

①-③Ice saws: (large, medium and small)④Pistal grip saw⑤Wide flat chisel⑥Medium flat chisel⑦Fine flat chisel⑧Small flat chisel⑨- ⑪ Angle chisels ⑫ Compass ⑬ Knife ⑭ Tape measure ⑮ Ice tongs ⑯ Tool bag

ANGLE CHISELS

There are many kinds of angle chisels, although not as many as the flat chisels.

- The large size has two blades, each 40 mm wide, with a distance of 80 mm between their edges. The handle is 150 mm long. This is a very versatile and useful tool.

The small size has two blades, each 20 mm wide, with a distance of 80 mm between their edges. The handle is 200 mm. This chisel is used to add the final lines to a piece.

ROUND CHISEL

This chisel is not needed by beginners.

KNIFE

A knife is sometimes necessary to remove small pieces of ice or to make small holes.

OTHER ITEMS

Both a compass and a ruler are convenient for the larger combined pieces. To start carving, you should have the following tools: (1) hand saws (large, medium, small) and a pistol-shaped saw, if possible; (2) flat chisels (large, medium, and small); (3) angle chisels (large and small); and (4) a knife.

ABOUT THE STAND

The stand for a small carving is about one-sixth of the size of the piece. For a standard carving, the stand is approximately 56 cm in length. For combined carvings, the standard size depends on the size of the carvings, but is actually somewhere around 2-3 mm long and 56 cm wide. The stands should have a drain. They are usually made of stainless steel or wood, and it is best to have a mat under the ice in the stand.

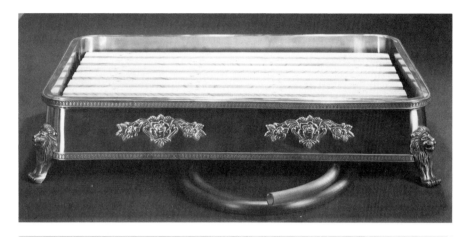

6. HOW TO HOLD THE ICE

- You should always wear gloves when working with ice.
- If the ice block is too large for you to hold by yourself, have an assistant help you or use a stand and a steel spear. However, the spear should be used carefully as sometimes the ice will break suddenly.

HOW TO CUT THE ICE

It is best to use a gasoline powered machine saw to make your cuts, but if one is unavailable, this method may be employed: place the ice in front of you, and cut it vertically, from top to bottom. It is best to cut in from both sides to get the most uniform finished block.

ICE SIZES

The standard cuts are shown on pages 10 and 11.

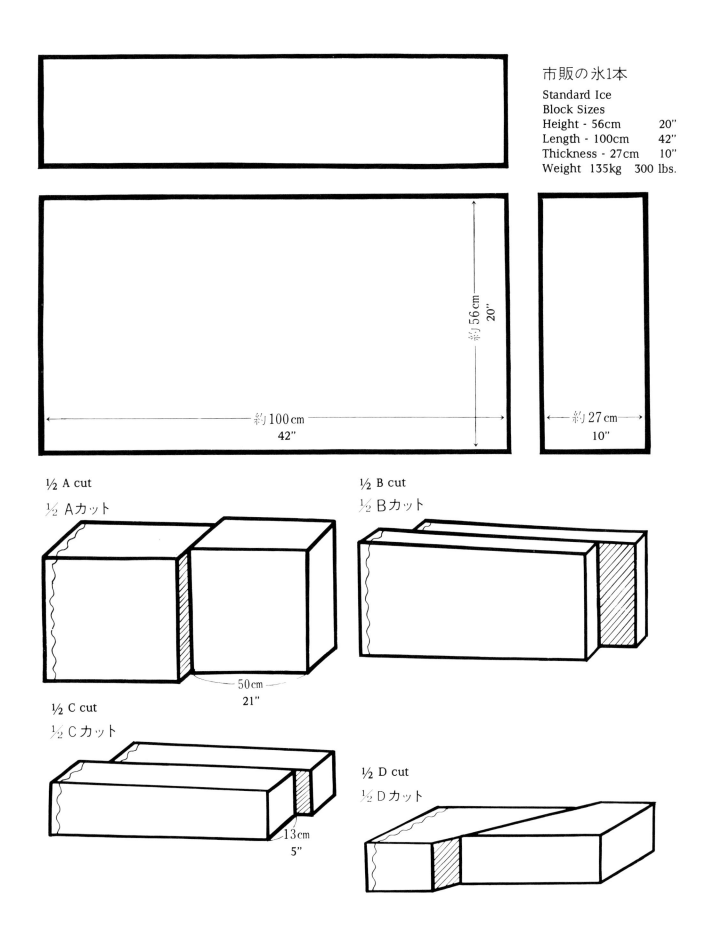

市販の氷1本
Standard Ice
Block Sizes

Height - 56cm	20"
Length - 100cm	42"
Thickness - 27cm	10"
Weight 135kg	300 lbs.

約56cm
20"

約100cm
42"

約27cm
10"

½ A cut

½ Aカット

½ B cut

½ Bカット

50cm
21"

½ C cut

½ Cカット

½ D cut

½ Dカット

13cm
5"

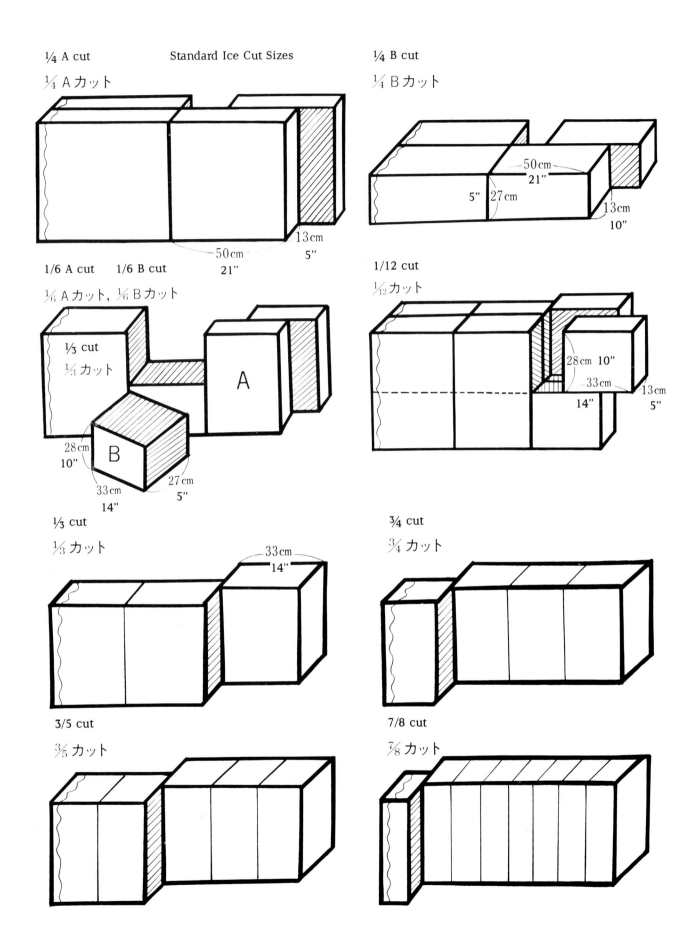

¼ A cut

¼ A カット

Standard Ice Cut Sizes

¼ B cut

¼ B カット

50 cm
21"
5"   27 cm
13 cm
10"

13 cm
5"
50 cm
21"

1/6 A cut   1/6 B cut

⅙ A カット, ⅙ B カット

⅓ cut

⅓ カット

A

B

28 cm
10"
33 cm
14"
27 cm
5"

1/12 cut

1/12 カット

28 cm 10"
33 cm
14"
13 cm
5"

⅓ cut

⅓ カット

33 cm
14"

¾ cut

¾ カット

3/5 cut

⅗ カット

7/8 cut

⅞ カット

7 SAFETY AND CARE OF TOOLS

Before you start cutting, you should carefully place the ice and your tools since they can sometimes become slippery and dangerous. The ice should be placed on a moveable wooden stand about as high as your hips. Your tools should be placed safely to one side. You should always wear gloves, as working with a chisel and cold hands is very dangerous, and water-proof shoes. The floor should have a dependable drainage system. When you work outside, you must be protected from both direct sunshine and wind. Since it takes beginners a long time tofinish a piece, I suggest you choose a simple subject such as a bowl. If you choose a difficult piece, the ice is likely to melt before you have finished.

Once you have finished working, your tools should be heated under hot water and dried. If you have time, you should sharpen the chisels as ice breaks easily under a dull blade. If these matters are taken care of before you start work, you will complete a better piece.

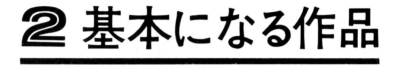

2 基本になる作品

BASIC PIECES

1 四角い容器

SQUARE DISH

Ice 1/12 Cut

This stylish square dish has a very large area at the bottom. It is practical to cool champagne or wine, or to use as a flower vase. It's pleasing appearance is achieved through its many lines.

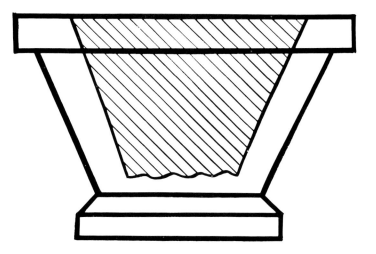

1

3

2

4

5

HOW TO CARVE

(1) Using a saw, square the ice, and plane off the excess with a flat chisel (photo 1).

(2) Smooth both the top and bottom with a hand saw (photo 2).

(3) Etch a line completely around the block a third up from the bottom (photo 3).

(4) At this point, cut into the ice to a depth of 1/6 of the block. Do not cut too deeply, and keep your eye on the blade (photo 4).

(5) From a point 1/5 from the top, cut down diagonally with the flat chisel so it meets the inside edge of the horizontal cut (photo 5).

(6) Turn the ice over, and 1/3 from the edge, cut lines parallel to the sides 1/8 through the block of ice. This will be the bottom.

(7) With the ice in this position, cut down diagonally as in Step 5, 1/3 from the top to meet the horizontal line cut in Step 4 (photo 6).

(8) Finish the bottom of the container cleanly, squaring off the edges (photo 7).

(9) Using a right-angle chisel, cut the acute inside angle on the base (photos 8 and 9).

6

7

8

9

10

11

(10) Turn the ice once again, and in the middle, draw a square 2/3 or 3/4 the size of the top with a flat chisel (photo 10). Then dig out the center cavity with the angle chisel (photos 11 and 12).

(11) Make inside surfaces proportionate to each other, then carve equally spaced flutings on the inside (photos 13 and 14).

(12) Turn the carving over and make similar fluting on the

12

13

14

15

16

17

outside (photo 15).
(13) Add another edge on the outside with the angle chisel
(photo 16).
(14) Carve flutings around the outside edges, finishing off

the carving (photo 17).

2 手付洋皿

SERVING TRAY WITH HANDLES

Ice 1/6 Cut

This piece has a wide range of uses as the bottom is hollow and wide. It can be used for various things, such as a tray for fruit, a display for melons or vegetables, and so on.

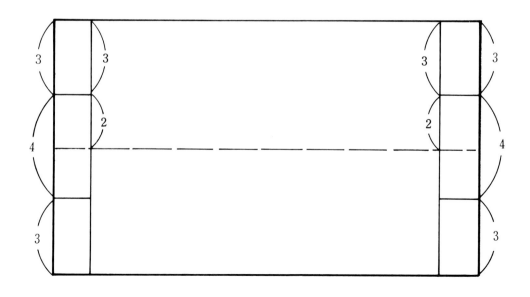

1

2

3

4

5

6

7

OBJECTIVE

The chief aim of this piece is practice in the technique of using the angle chisel for smoothing; you must be very careful. To do this, the angle chisel is held horizontally. The difficult part is making the handle, but if it is done like sharpening a pencil, there should not be any great mistakes.

8

9

10

11

12

13

HOW TO CARVE

(1) Cut the ice into a rectangle, and square the surface of the ice. Make a 60° angle on the sides to make the handle (photos 1, 2, and 3).

(2) Leaving 5 cm from left and right sides, make parallel lines to a depth of 1/2 that of the block (photo 4).

(3) Stand the ice on first one side, and cut the bottom of the dish parallel with the flat chisel (photos 5, 6, and 7). Laying the dish down, you should trim off the thickness of the handles.

(4) Shape the handle, cutting away the excess with the saw (photo 9), then finish the thickness of the handles with the

14

15

16

17

18

19

flat chisel.
(5) Bevel the outside edges (photo 10).
(6) Etch four lines 5 cm from each side in the top, and with the angle chisel, dig this out parallel to the outside bevel (photos 11 and 12)
(7) With a flat chisel, make the bottom flat, and with the angle chisel smooth out the beveled inside edges (photos 13, 14, and 15).
(8) Carve the handles and make the holes with a knife and a angle chisel (photos 16 and 17).
(9) Carve flutings around the circumference with the angle chisel (photos 18 and 19).

③ 丸い器
ROUND BOWL

Ice ¼ A Cut

This is a low bowl, with eight arcs carved on it. It is good with seasonal fruit or salads, and is interesting with flower arrangements (with flower arrangements, the bottom should be thicker). The eight identical arcs are cut geometrically to avoid distortion of the round bowl.

1

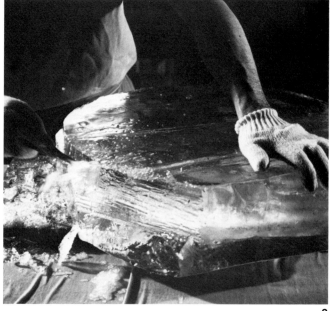

2

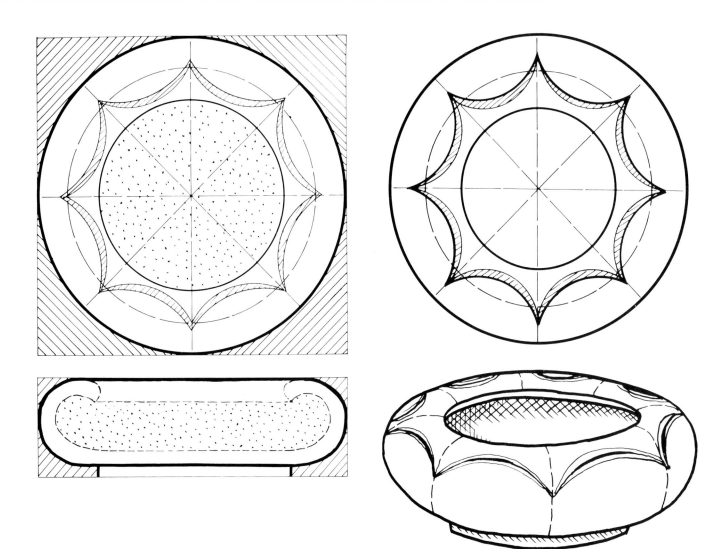

HOW TO CARVE

(1) Square the sides with the flat chisel.
(2) Measure the ice with the saw, or tape, and make an octagonal figure etching the shape with a small flat chisel and cutting off the four corners with the saw (photo 1).
(3) Make 8 circles on the sides with a small flat chisel, touching edge to edge.

(4) Deepen the circles with the small chisel (photo 2).
(5) After etching the circles on the top, carve out a cylinder with a large or medium flat chisel, working from top to bottom (photo 3).
(6) Etch a circle of 1/2 to 2/3 of the radius of the cylinder using the same center point, with a small flat chisel (photo 4).

3

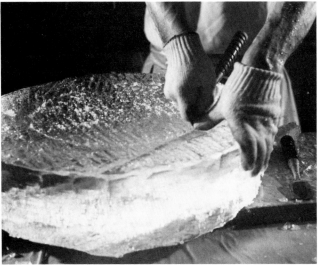

4

5

6

7

8

(7) After making sure that the circle is accurate, cut the circle deeper with the angle chisel. This will be the bottom of the bowl (photo 5).

(8) Make a line around the circumference about 2 to 3 cm in from the top with the small flat chisel (photo 6).

(9) Cut through this line horizontally until the inner circle is met (photo 7).

(10) Remove the excess ice by cutting down horizontally with the flat chisel to the saw cut (photo 8). Place the flat chisel parallel to the ice so it will not dig in too deeply.

(11) Square the bottom of the bowl with the angle chisel.

9

10

11

12

13

(12) Round the sides, working from the bottom to the sides, and dig out the middle of the bottom. Turn the piece over, and using the same method as for the bottom, work the rounded edge to the inner circle (photos 9, 10, and 11).

(13) Dig out the circle that was etched on the top with both the flat chisel and the angle chisel on the bottom. The thickness of the bottom is about 2 to 3 cm (photo 12).

(14) Shape the outside of the bowl with the saw, and the border with the angle chisel (photo 13).

(15) Make 8 semi-circles with the flat chisel. Make sure that each semi-circle has the same size and depth. Shape the lines with the angle chisel.

14

4 広縁丸型容器

WIDE-LIPPED DISH

Ice 1/12 Cut

This is a bowl with a wide rim. The lines of this bowl are beautiful, giving the elegant feeling of cut crystal. It is not particularly difficult for a beginner, but the piece requires some skill. From the practice on this piece with the flat chisel, in the cutting of a cylinder, you will get to know the characteristics of the flat chisel.

HOW TO CARVE

(1) Make the top and bottom level, mark out a full circle and cut off the excess. You should start with a regular octagon (photo 1).
(2) Complete the circular shape on top, and, with a small chisel, work down vertically to the bottom to form a cylinder (photo 3).
(3) Mark a line around the cylinder and 1/4 from the bottom. This will be the thickness of the edge.
(4) Cut in horizontally until 1/4 of the radius is reached (photo 4).
(5) On the top, etch a circle 1/2 the radius with the angle chisel. This will be the bottom (photo 5).
(6) From this circle, cut down at an angle to the saw cut (Step 4) (photo 6). Exercise moderation in making the downward cuts, and do not cut too much.

1

2

3

4

5

6

7

8

9

10

11

12

(7) Carefully square and shape the outside surface and edge with the flat chisel or angle chisel (photo 7).

(8) Turn the ice over, and on the surface draw a circle 2/3 the radius of the outside edge.

(9) Carefully carve out the center of the circle. Make the bottom flat (photo 8).

(10) Turn the ice over again, and using the single chisel, shape the lines of the outsides and under-lip (photo 9).

(11) Turn the piece over once again, and do the same to the outside lip (photos 10 and 11). In this instance, you should not only use the angle chisel, but you should also use the triangle chisel for the proper shape of the flutings.

(12) Turn the piece over and finish off as necessary (photo 12).

5 丸型手付容器

A ROUND DISH WITH HANDLES

Ice 1/12 Cut

The handles on this beautiful, curved dish should be large.

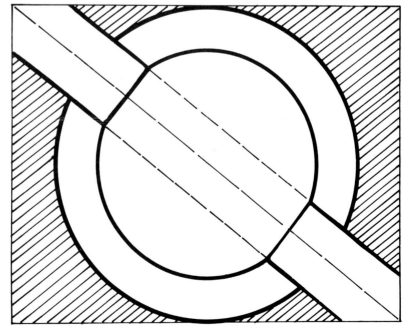

1

2

3

4

5

6

HOW TO CARVE

(1) The top and bottom of the rectangular block should be flat.

(2) Etch a circle on the top of the ice, then etch a diagonal line through the center of the circle, from opposite corners. Then etch two handle outlines using the diagonal as a center line (photo 1).

(3) Deepen the lines with an angle chisel (photo 2).

(4) Cut away the excess ice from the sides and handles with the flat chisel (photo 3).

(5) Cut the lines with the saw, as shown in picture #4, 1/5 of the thickness of the ice (photo 5), and etch a line between the two handle saw cuts.

7   8

9   10

11   12

(6) Clear away the ice between these two cuts (photo 6).

(7) Cut away the remaining ice from the handles (photo 7).

(8) Square the shape of the handles (photos 8 and 9).

(9) Shape the left and right handles properly.

(10) Etch the inside circles on both handles, and cut out the ice for the main center cavity (photos 10 and 11).

(11) Cut out the circles in the center of the handles with a small angle chisel (photos 12, 13, and 14).

(12) Supporting the ice with your left hand by the edge of the table, carve the flutings down to the bottom of the bowl.

13

14

15

16

17

18

(13) Next, make similar decorations on the inside (photos 15, 16, and 17).

(14) Carve a single line around the handles (photo 18).

⑥ 葉型容器

A LEAF-SHAPED DISH

A leaf is not an interesting figure in itself, so this one is designed in a curve, with the handle formed from the stem so the figure will be well balanced. As the end of the stem curves over the leaf, it is important in achieving a balanced form so the edges of the leaf point outward.

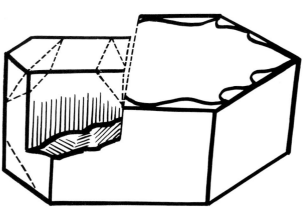

HOW TO CARVE

(1) Etch the shape of the bottom with a flat chisel, and cut the rough shape with a hand saw (photo 1).

(2) Cut down 2/5 through the block at the point of the stem (photo 2).

(3) Cut away the ice from both sides of the stem with the flat chisel and angle chisel (photo 3).

(4) Cut out the shape of the leaf, working from the point of the leaf to the stem (photos 4 and 5).

(5) After cutting out the shape of the leaf, round off the stem (photo 6).

(6) Cut the stem so the curve just touches the dish (photo 7), and shape the contour of the leaf.

6

7

8

9

10

11

(7) Roughly shape the inside of the dish, and then make a 5 cm cut at the end of the stem (photo 9).

(8) Round the stem proportionally, and then bore out a hole with a small flat chisel (photos 10 and 11).

(9) Determine the finished design and shape the inside with an angle chisel (photo 12). At this time, carefully form the inside bottom.

(10) Holding the piece in one hand, make the final outside lines with a small angle chisel (photo 13).

(11) Clean the hole of the stem, which is now the handle, with a knife, and add the final touches with the flat chisel (photo 14).

(12) Make the inside lines with the small angle chisel (photos 15 and 16).

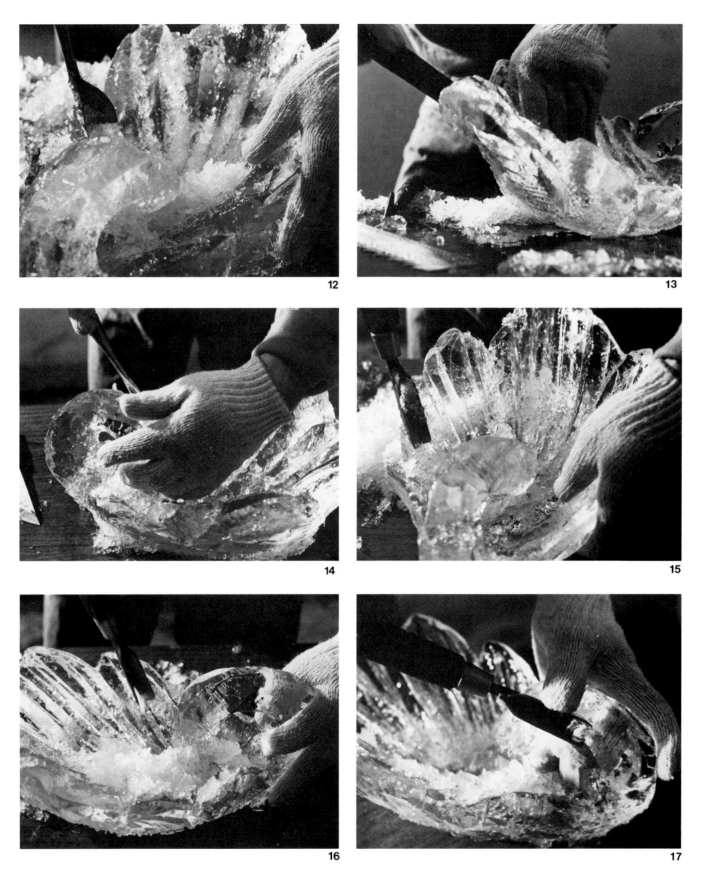

12 **13** **14** **15** **16** **17**

(13) Shape the detail of the whole leaf and make the curves
uniform, inside and out, with a triangle chisel.

7 貝の皿

A SHELL-SHAPED DISH

Ice 1/6 A Cut

Ice 1/6 A Cut

As this shell-shaped dish has many facet-like cuts on its surface, the reflections of light are very pretty. Also, due to its shell-like shape, it can be used for serving cold cuts (sashimi) or the like.

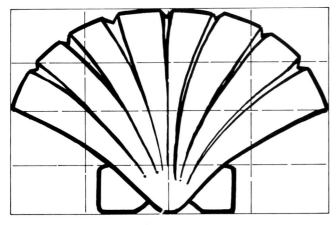

HOW TO CARVE

(1) First, draw the lines of the shell on the total surface area of the ice. Notice that left and right sides are symmetrical (photo 1).

(2) Cut each edge roughly with the hand saw (photos 2 and 3), then draw an outline of the shell with the flat chisel (photo 4).

(3) In a smooth curve, etch a line marking the halfway point across the thickness of the hinge of the shell, and then deepen the line with the angle chisel (photos 5 and 6).

(4) Round the shell, working from the mouth towards the

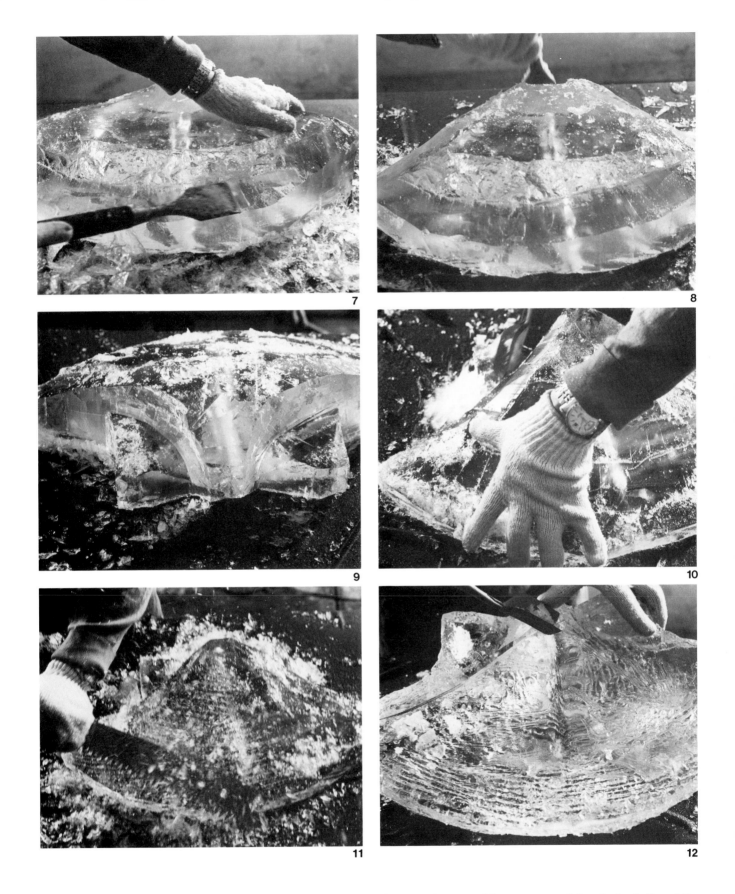

7

8

9

10

11

12

hinge. Take note of the symmetry of the whole shell, and the fact that the hinge edge is thicker than the mouth; do not cut too deeply (photos 8 and 9).

(5) Round the edges of the hinge, so the shape is slightly oval (photo 10).

(6) Shape the surface of the shell with a hand saw (photo 11).

13

14

15

16

(7) Turn the shell over, and shape the edges of the shell from the hinge to the mouth. Then dig out the center area, leaving the shell at the proper thickness (photos 12 and 13).

(8) With the angle chisel, carve the flutings in the center (Photo 14). Carve the flutings on each side symmetrically (photo 15).

(9) Turn the shell over, and carve the flutings between the ones on the other side (photo 16).

(10) Be sure to use the angle chisel in cutting the flutings (photo 17).

17

⑧ 形の組合せ
COMBINATION OF FIGURES

Ice 1/16 A Cut

This piece demonstrates the interesting forms of the variations of a bird's wing, combined with arabesque design. It is a little difficult for beginners, but it is a good basic piece for practice in using the chisel and saw.

1

2

3

4

CARVING POINTERS

Flat chisels, angle chisels and a hand saw are used at different times, and you should know when to use each of them properly. Also, you should observe how to hold and how to use the chisels from the pictures, and note the placement of left and right hands.

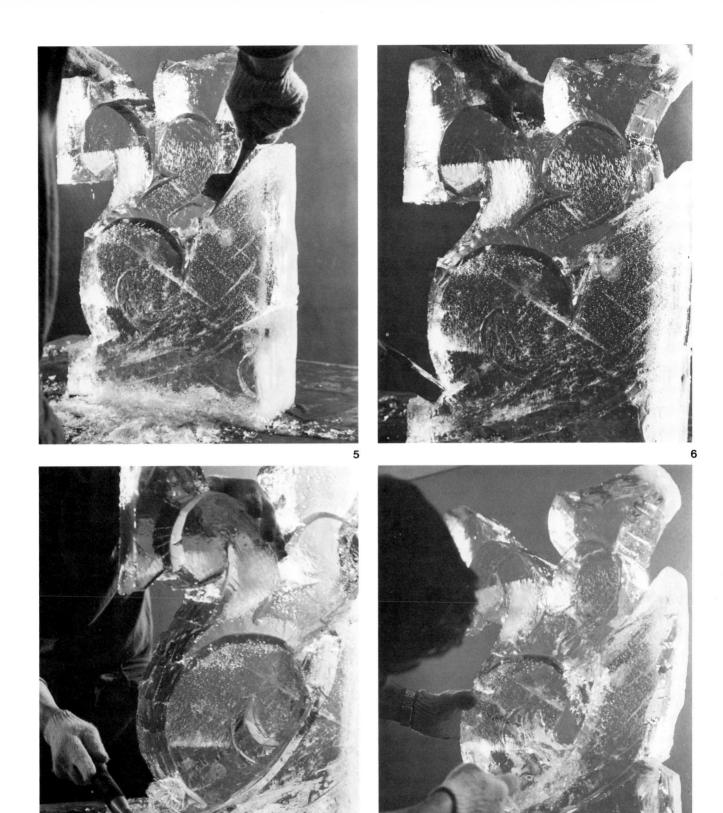

5

6

7

8

HOW TO CARVE

(1) Etch the basic lines with a small flat chisel (photo 1), then deepen them (photo 2).

(2) Cut out the basic shape with the saw (photo 3).

(3) If you cannot use the hand saw, use the small flat chisel (photo 4).

(4) Using the angle chisel, completely cut out the contours (photo 5).

(5) Square the base of the figure with the flat chisel and the angle chisel (photos 6 and 7).

(6) Using a narrow flat chisel, cut the hole in the center, and then widen the hole to the proper size (photo 8).

9

10

11

12

(7) Using the angle chisel, work the upper sections to the correct thickness (photo 9).

(8) If the chisel cannot be used, use the saw slowly to cut off the ice (photo 10). This is a useful technique, so it would be well to master it (photo 11).

(9) Shape the figure, using the flat and angle chisels alternately (photos 12 and 13). To make smooth lines use the

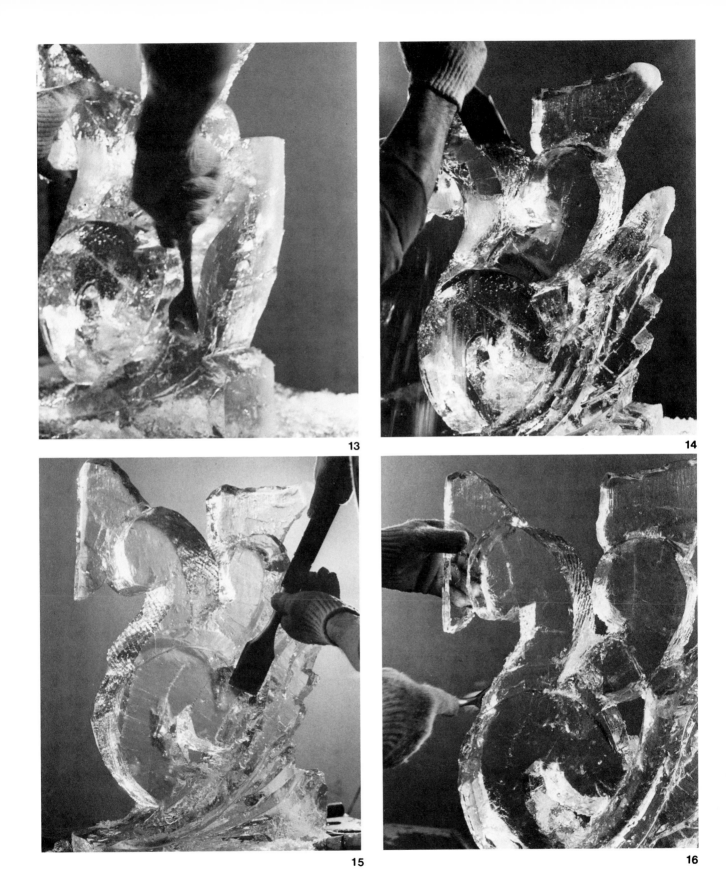

13

14

15

16

tip of the chisel for carving (photos 14 and 15). You have to use the flat and the angle chisel alternately to shape the piece. As there are many of curving lines, and there is extensive use of the angle chisel, this piece perfectly shows the curving lines that are the characteristic feature of the angle chisel (photos 16 and 17).

17

18

19

20

(10) When doing the detail work, take off thin shavings of ice to bring out the feeling of the piece (photos 18, 19, and 20). When cutting smooth curving lines, it is important to coordinate the left hand with the right when using the chisels, particularly the small flat chisel. This basic technique must be practiced with care; otherwise, you cannot adequately develop the feeling of the piece.

❸ 初級作品

BEGINNING PIECES

1 手 桶

JAPANESE STYLE BUCKET

Ice ½ A Cut

One does not often see this kind of bucket in Japan nowadays, but when it is used as a decoration in wedding receptions in Japan, it helps create a classic Japanese atmosphere. The handle is about the same height as the bucket, and the hoops of the bucket are round.

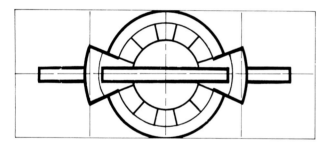

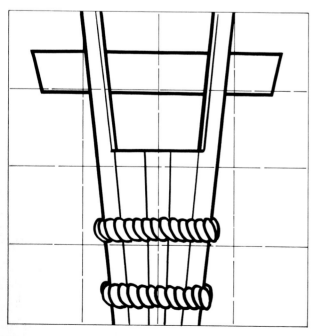

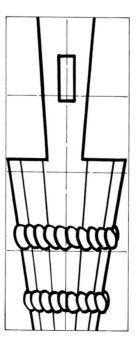

HOW TO CARVE

(1) Draw the rough shape on the ice, and cut away the excess (photo 1).

(2) Using the flat chisel, cut out the handles and the space between them (photos 2, 3, and 4).

(3) Roughly shape the whole piece, and decide upon how thick you want the handles (photos 5 and 6).

(4) Gradually work the handles to the proper thickness, from the insides (photos 7 and 8).

(5) Decide on the width of the handles, then cut out the excess ice with the saw and the flat chisel (photos 9 and 10).

(6) Shape the upright and the cross support of the handle. Square the joint between the upright and the cross support (photo 11).

(7) Round the bucket (photos 12 and 13). Remember that the individual hoops on the bucket should stand out.

7

8

9

10

11

(8) After shaping the outside, carve out the inside, making sure the depth at the bottom is uniform (photo 14).
(9) Finish the details of the bucket, squaring all the edges

12

14

13

15

16

and corners (photo 15).
(10) Carve the strands in the rope hoops around the bucket
with the angle chisel (photo 16).

② リボン付かご
BASKET WITH A RIBBON

Ice ¼ A Cut

This basket is accented with a decorative ribbon on the handle. It has a nice effect when filled with flowers or fruit for simple cocktail or tea parties.

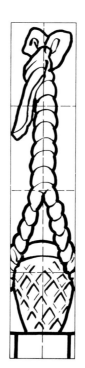

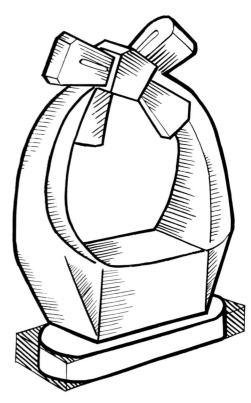

50

1

2

HOW TO CARVE

(1) Etch the outline, and cut out the contours (photos 1 and 2).

(2) Put the ice on its side, and cut the hole between the handle and the basket. Cut the hole so you have enough ice remaining for proper rounding off and trimming (photos 3 and 4).

4

3

5

6

7

9

8

10

(3) Form the shape of the handle, working up from the basket, gradually working the handle thinner towards the ribbon (photo 5). This is done by alternately working on each side of the piece.

11

12

(4) Shape the outside of the basket, then work up the inside of the handle, separating the two ends of the ribbon (photos 6 – 10).

(5) Finish the final shaping of the basket, being careful not to make the sides of the cavity too thin (photos 11 and 12).

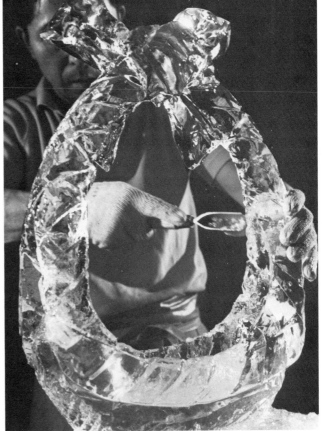

14

(6) After the basket is fully shaped, carve the decorative lines on the basket and finish the ribbon (photos 13 and 14).

13

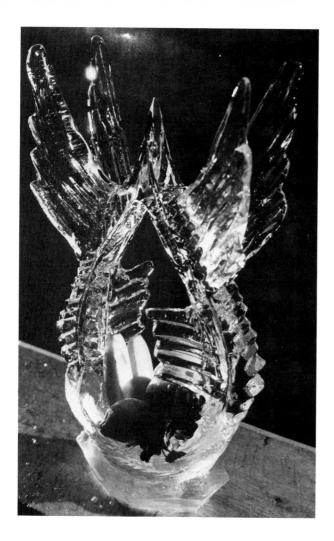

③ 羽付かご
WINGED BASKET

Ice 1/6 Cut

The handle of this basket is decorated with wings. The same techniques as in the previous basket are used, but making the wings is a delicate job. When carving the wings, keep the over-all balance in mind, and this piece will become a thing of beauty.

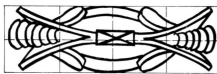

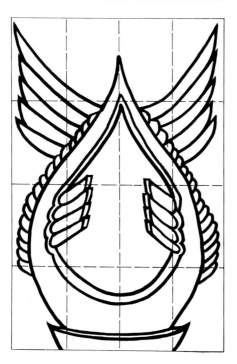

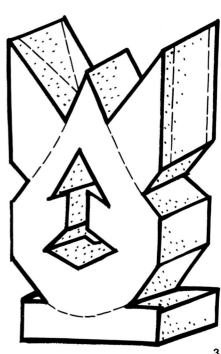

3

1

2

4

5

HOW TO CARVE

● Make the rough outline on the ice, of patterns 3 and 6 with reference to photos 1-7, using the preceeding exercise as a guide to the essential steps.

● When etching the shape of the wing, as in photographs 8 and 9, support the piece with one hand and carve gently with shallow cuts.

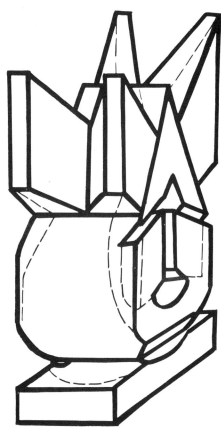

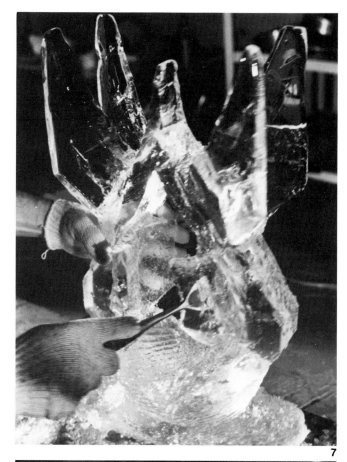

6

7

8

9

● After the outline of the wings are shaped, use the angle chisel to finish them. Each wing should be tapered slightly, so the upper edges are thinner.

4 ふた付鍋
PAN AND COVER

Ice 2 pieces, each 1/12 Cut

In adding a lid to this pan, the whole appearance is changed. This is useful, as Japanese cooking such as soba, somen (Japanese cold noodles), or even salads will go quite nicely in this. It is important that the inside and outside sides of the pan are smooth, regular, and of even thickness.

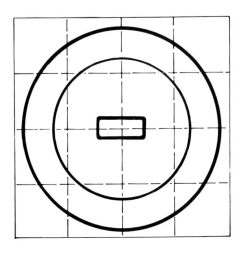

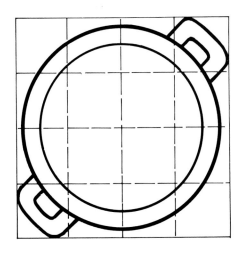

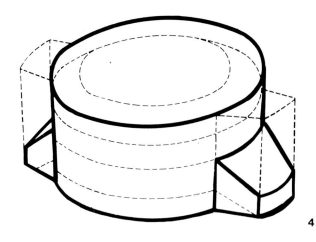

1

4

2

5

3

6

HOW TO CARVE
(1) Smoothen both sides of the ice, and etch a full circle on the upper side. Include the area for the handles, and then cut away the excess ice (photos 1-7).
(2) To make the handles, cut down 1/3 from the top, and form the handles as in photos 9-11.

(3) Remove the ice from the inside of the pan (photo 12).
(4) Make the holes in the handles of both the pan and lid with a knife (photo 13).

13

16

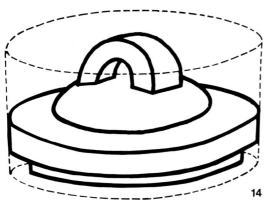

14

17

(5) To keep errors to a minimum, use the flat chisel in marking the sides.
(6) Use the same size circle to make the lid, leaving enough ice for the knob. Finish the ornamental lines (photos 15-18).

15

18

5 コーヒーポット

COFFEE POT

Ice 1/6 A Cut

There are a lot of rather ordinary looking coffee pots, so I designed this one especially for ice carving. It imparts a classical feeling in the legs and in the variations in the lid.

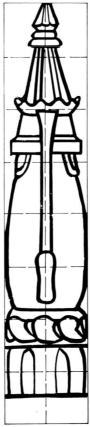

HOW TO CARVE
- When forming the body, make the shape as full as possible, with the handle and spout balancing each other.

1

2

3

4

● Etch the shape of the pot, cut away the excess ice, and shape from top to bottom, leaving the handle and spout until last (photos 1-8).

● After shaping the body, finish the stand and legs by measuring the length one at a time from the bottom of the pot, and then removing the ice from between the legs (photo 9).

5

6

7

8

9

⑥ 花びん
FLOWER VASE

Ice 1/6 A Cut

This piece is made by combining a horn and a circle, and is a perfect subject for practice in developing these shapes.

1

2

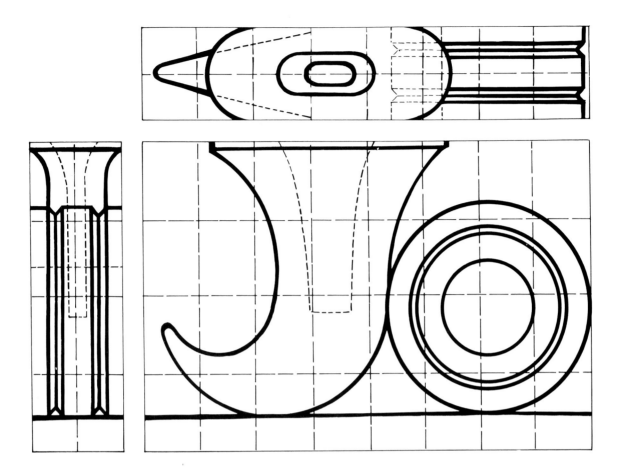

HOW TO CARVE

- Make the circle perfectly round. Be sure the rough draft is correctly drawn, as it is important for finished work to be faithful to the plan. Be careful that the circle does not become oval (photos 1-4).
- When developing the shape of the horn, remember that from the mouth, it tapers gradually to a point (photos 4 and 8).
- The inside of the horn expands outward, so care must be taken to avoid damaging the edge (photos 5 and 6).
- The area between the horn and the circle should be cut away below and above the circle (photos 7 and 9).
- In finishing, make sure the curves are symmetrical (photo 10).

3

4

5

6

7

8

9

10

7 バスケット

BASKET

Ice 1/6 A Cut

This basket has a simple design, without any decoration such as wings or a ribbon. Therefore, it is important to keep an overall balance in it's form and decorative cuts.

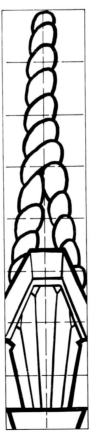
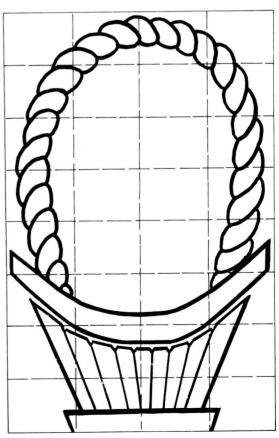

1

2

3

4

5

HOW TO CARVE

- The handle of this basket is larger than the others, so the balance of the shape should always be kept in mind; the final result should be like that of weaving (photos 1-10).
- The basic technique is the same as that for the basket

6

7

8

9

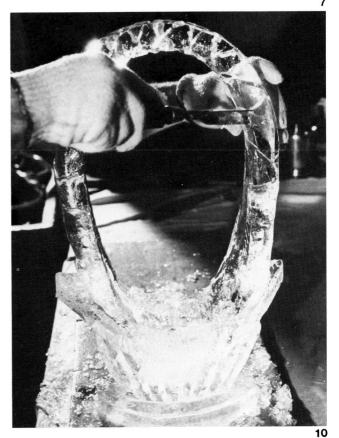

10

with wings and the basket with the ribbon.
● When using the chisel to bring out the texture of weaving, carve gently with the angle chisel. Support the piece with your other hand (photo 10).

⑧ 扇

FAN

Ice 1/6 A Cut

This neatly cut fan evokes a pure Japanese atmosphere. It is very effective in beautifully displaying sashimi, vegetables, fruits, and cold hors d'oeuvres, particularly in Japanese-style banquets.

1

2

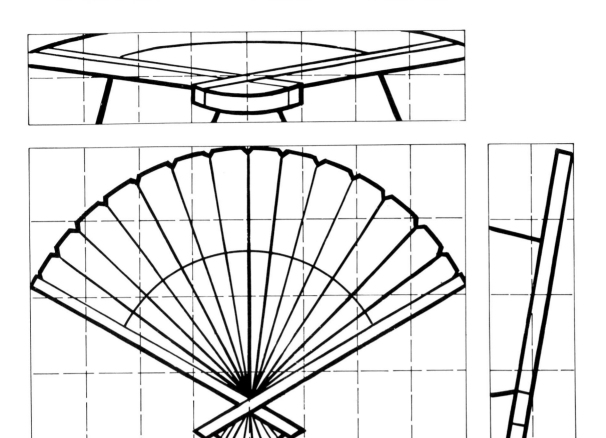

HOW TO CARVE

- When making the rough draft, think of the fan as part paper, part bamboo, and part handle, with the bamboo part wider than the others. The stand is an extension of the bamboo part.
- Slightly bevel the paper part, working towards the outer edge. The center of the bamboo part is about 1/3 the thickness of the ice from the top.

3

5

4

6

7

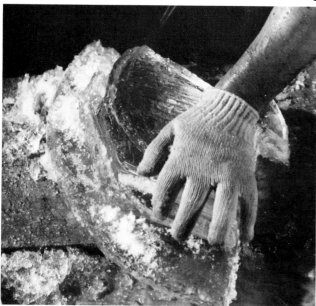

9

8

10

11

● The paper part is worked alternately on the top and bottom, beveling in a straight line using the flat chisel, from the tip of the fan in towards the handle. Finish the folds on the fan, making about 14 of them. Note that the folds should overlap to the right, radiating out from the center.

12

15

13

16

● Photos 7-10 show how to cut the stand, photos 11, 12, and 16 show how to cut the folds on the paper parts, and photo 13 shows how to cut the folds for reflection under the stand. Photograph 15 shows how to cut folds in the handle while photograph 14 shows how to trim the ice underneath the handle. Photograph 17 shows how to cut the folds in the bamboo part.

17

14

18

⑨ 帆かけ舟

JAPANESE SAIL BOAT

Ice ½ A Cut

This is a representation of a type of Japanese sailboat during the Edo period, 1603 to 1869. You should endeavor to show this ocean-going vessel's graceful power through its billowing sail.

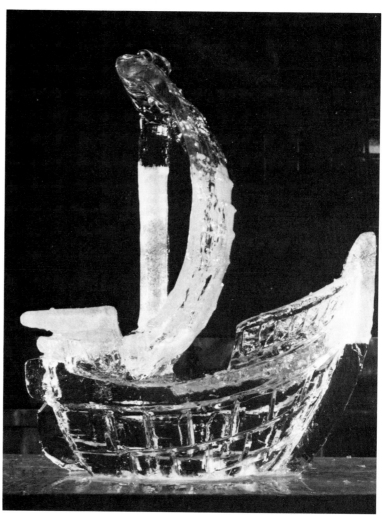

HOW TO CARVE

- With this piece, cut out the shape with a saw after etching the outline.
- Cut out the bow and both sides of ship (photos 2-5). Note that from bow to stern there is an accentuated sheer line, with the topsides made of long thin planks.

1

2

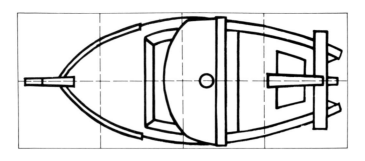

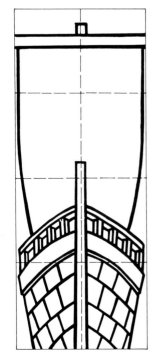

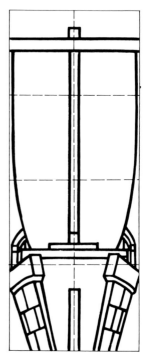

3

4

5

7

6

8

- The sail billows out towards the bow, and the center of the sail at the top is attached to the mast (photos 6-8).
- Cut out the space between the mast and the sail. The thickness of the sail should be constant, and the mast should be thicker than the sail (photos 7 and 8).
- Make lines on the hull to simulate planking.

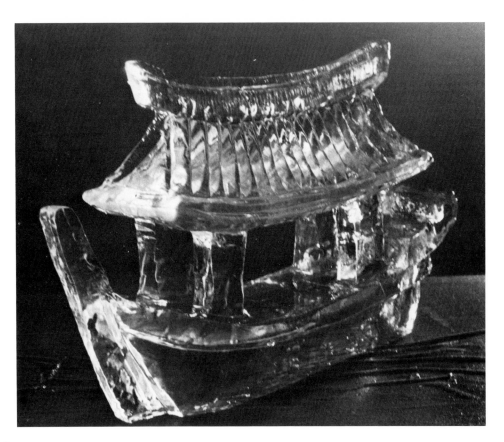

10 屋形船

JAPANESE HOUSEBOAT

Ice 1/6 A Cut

This type of barge was used by the nobility for sight-seeing excursions on the larger rivers and lakes. It shows a refined elegance in its form and balance.

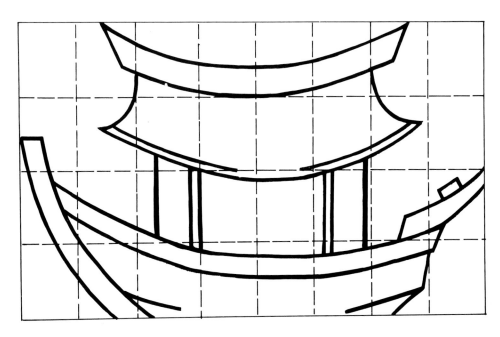

1

4

2

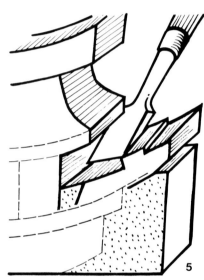

5

HOW TO CARVE

- In etching the outline, refer to Excercise 9, a Japanese Sailboat.
- Bring out the feeling of the boat by the varied flutings on the roof and by its bow shape (photos 1, 2, and 16). When done properly, the fluting and the bow give an overall excellent finished effect.

- Carefully etch the four roof pillars on the ice, making sure they are opposite to one another in relation to the deck. They should be square, and are best made with the angle chisel. Next, cut the fore and aft parts of the boat. In the last step, cut out the ice between the roof pillars (photos 13-15).

3

6

7

8

9

10

11

12

13

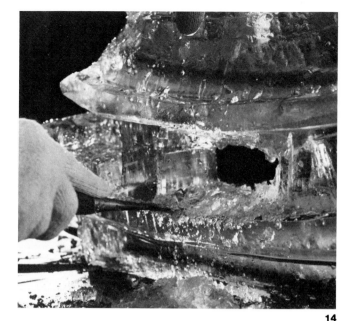

14

15

16

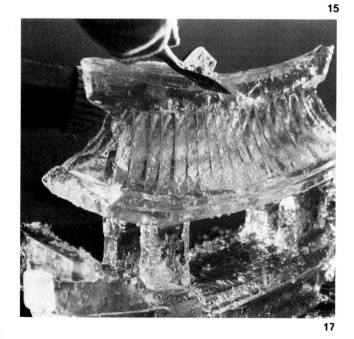

17

18

4 中級作品

INTERMEDIATE PIECES

1 ばしょうかじき

SWORDFISH

Ice 1/6 A Cut

There are a lot of possible variations in the shape of the swordfish, any one of which could be chosen as a point of emphasis. One theme which can easily become a distinctive feature is the expression of freedom in the flowing lines of the fish. The sharp sword, the large head, and the somewhat conical body, and the chest, back, and tail should be emphasized. This is the moment the fish is hooked, so the fins are fully spread out.

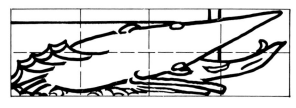

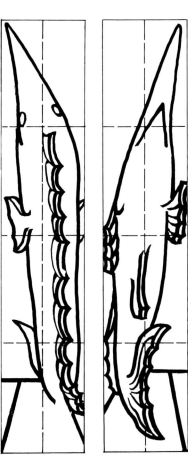

HOW TO CARVE
(1) Etch the shape of the fish on the ice, after carefully studying the four drawings.
(2) Cut out the shape with the saw, removing the unused ice. Then working down from the head with the chisel, make the rounded head and the sword (photos 1 and 2).
(3) Working on the back, bring out the full shape of the fin, making a clear line where the dorsal fin joins the body (photos 3 and 4).

1

4

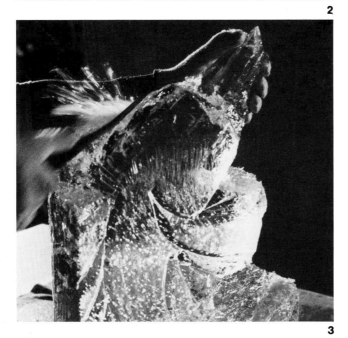

2

5

3

(4) Make the torso, chest, tail, and fins, emphasing these lines (photo 5).
(5) Cut out the sword, and make the mouth (photo 6).

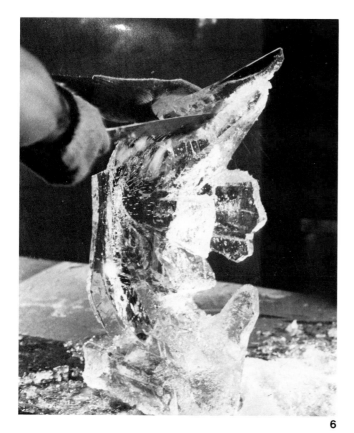

6

7

8

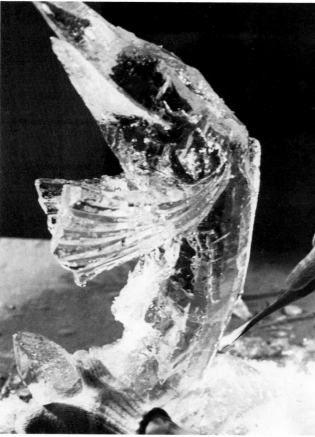

9

10

(6) Using the angle chisel, carve the lines in the fins, working on alternate sides (photos 7 and 8).
(7) Shape the body, from the head toward the tail, emphasing the strength of these lines (photos 9-11).

11

12

14

13

15

(8) Finish the tail and the body with the saw (photos 12 and 13).

(9) Finish the tail and back. Make the lines from tail to head, and on the dorsal fin.

(10) Finish the sword and mouth (photos 14 and 15).

2 龍の落し子

SEA HORSE

Ice ¼ A Cut

This is a representation of a sea horse which swims upright. The head is at a right angle to the body the tail is curved inward, and it looks somewhat like a reptile. The distinctive feature is that it is delicate to carve.

1

4

2

5

3

HOW TO CARVE
- Be very careful when etching the sea horse, making sure the shape is balanced (photo 1).
- Photos 2-6 show the rough cuts, and photo 7 shows some of the detail cuts.

6

7

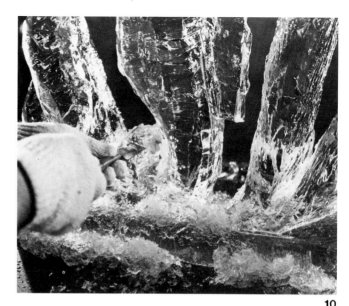

10

8

11

9

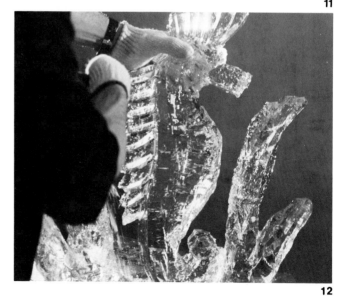

12

● To develop the feeling of the seaweed swaying in the surge, the length, thickness and width of each stem varies, to keep the overall balance of the piece in mind (photos 1 and 17). It would be good to refer to the "Angel Fish's" head.

13

14

15

16

17

18

● When doing the body of the sea horse, use the angle chisel to bring out the scales and fins (photo 15). Do the stand last (photo 18).

③ かごかき鯛

RED SNAPPER

Ice ¼ A Cut

This is a favorite Japanese fish. There are quite a few fish in this species. The characteristic points are the sharp back fin and the full body. These fish are seen from the beaches of Hawaii and Australia, and can be seen in Japanese coastal waters in the summer. In this piece, the dorsal fin is emphasized.

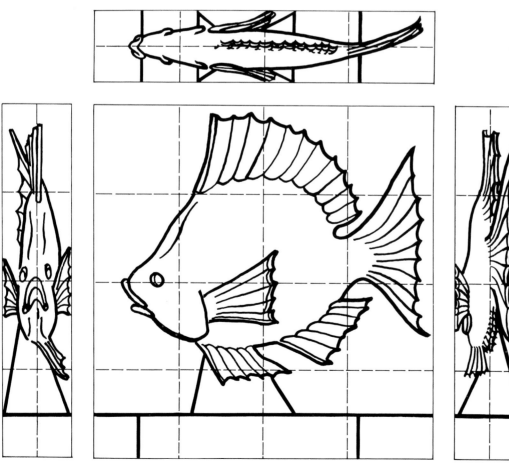

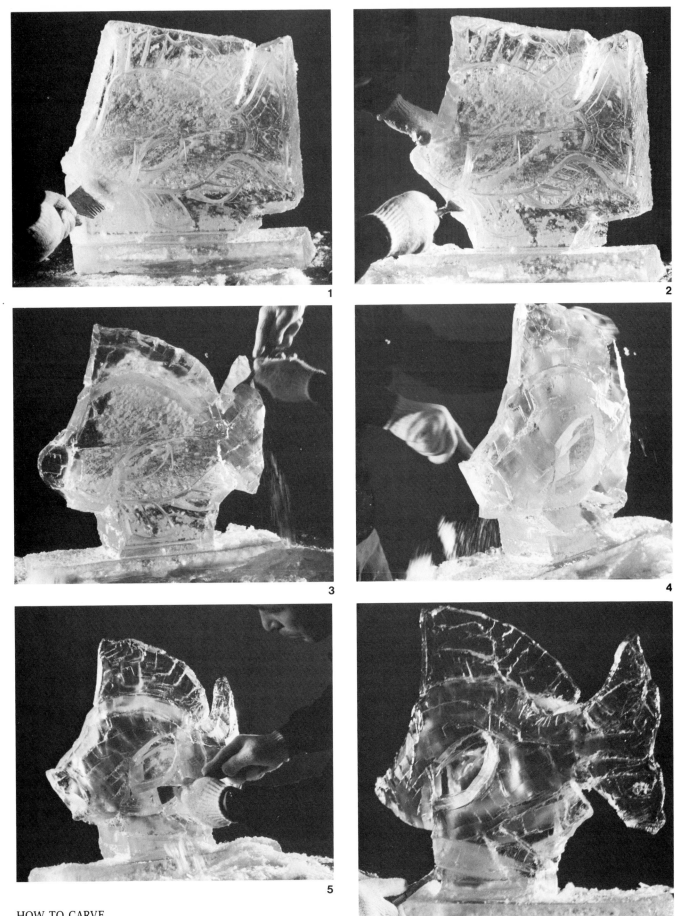

HOW TO CARVE
● The fish is curved, to emphasize the fins and oval body shape.

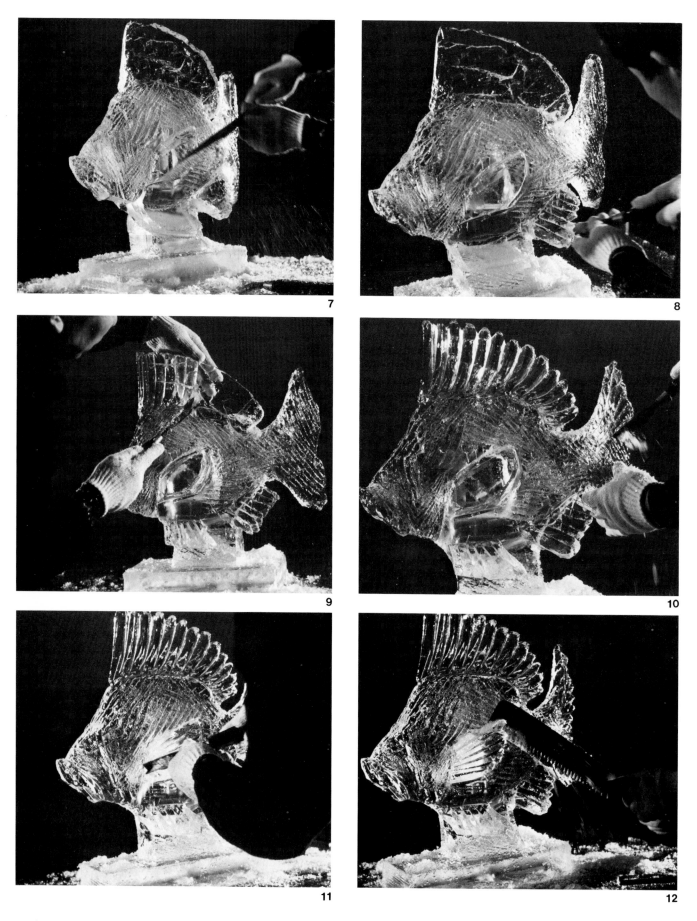

7

8

9

10

11

12

● Photos 1-6 show the roughing out procedure, finishing with the saw. Each fin must be done carefully as they are the main points of the piece (photos 8-12).

● It is important to do the pectoral fins last, as they are touching the stand.

4 ねずみ
MOUSE

Ice 1/6 A Cut

In this piece, the negative image of the mouse is countered by emphasing its charm. To do this, the mouse is perched on a wheel, with its forefeet raised. Also, the tail is long and curving.

1

2

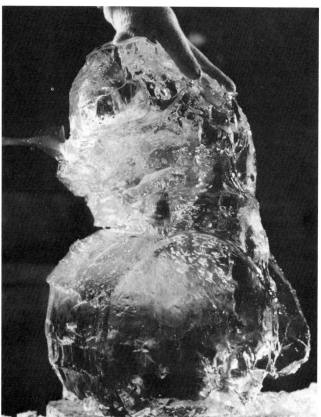

3

4

HOW TO CARVE

- Divide the ice into two equal sections, and make the rough draft of the mouse and wheel as full as possible, keeping the balance of the piece in mind. Look at it as a group of balanced circles.

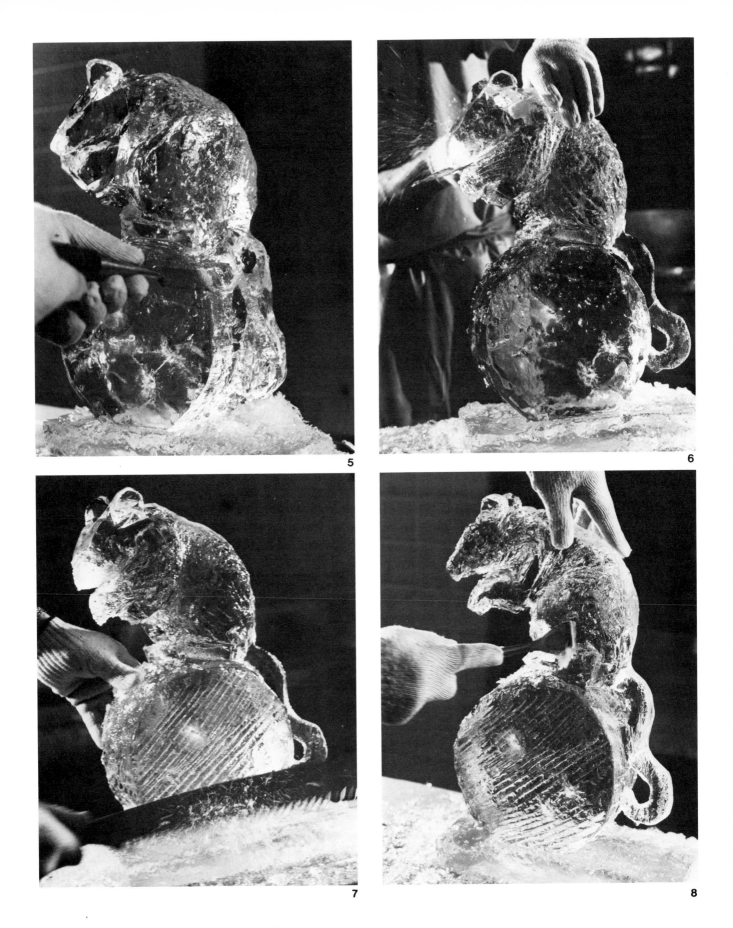

5

6

7

8

● As in other animals, a characteristic of the mouse is its clutched front feet. The head of the mouse is small, with a sharp nose, and small cute ears. These features will make the sculpture a success (photos 1-7).

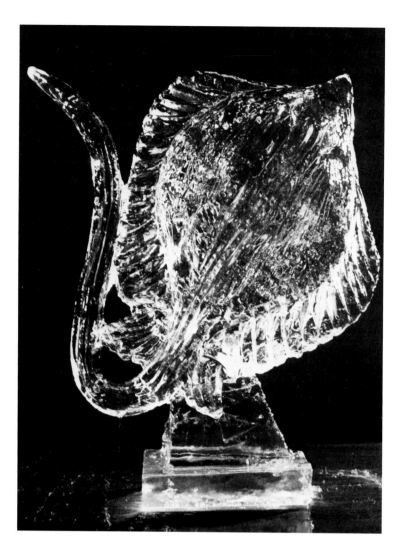

5 あかえい
STINGRAY

Ice ¼ A Cut

The stingray has an unusual flat shape, with a long slender tail. The shape is decidedly different from that of a normal fish, and it is easy to emphasize the stingray's particular beauty.

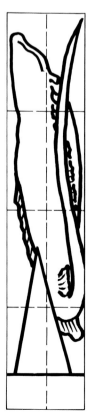
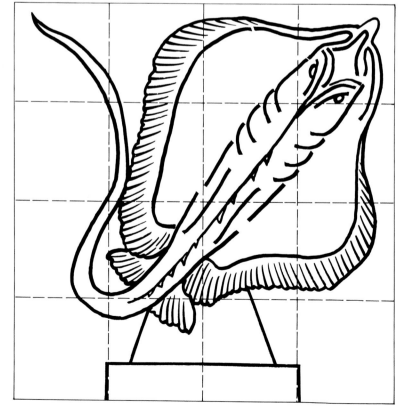

1

2

HOW TO CARVE

● The body of the stingray is thick, thinning down towards the edges, the fins being even thinner. The back is smooth and curved, but the underside is flat and has a face-like figure.

3

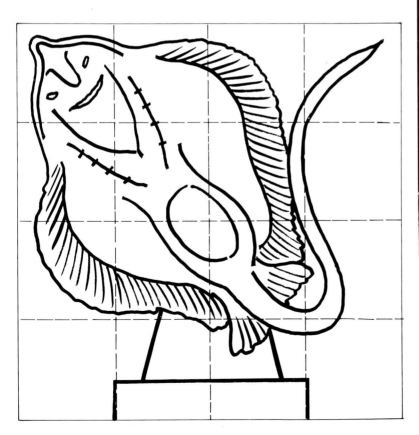

4

7

5

8

6

- The body is cut out from head to tail with a saw; the tail is an extension of the backbone ridge (photos 1-8).

9

12

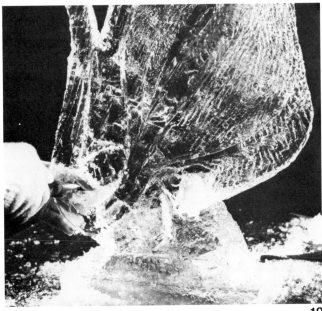

10

13

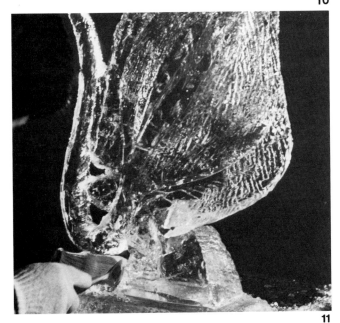

11

• Use the angle chisel when working on the body and fins.
Finish the piece by bringing out the details (photos 9-12).

⑥ 般若の面

MASK OF THE DEVIL

Ice 1/6 A Cut

This mask can be said to generally resemble those made by the monks of the Nara period (710-794), when this city was the cultural and political capital of Japan. The characteristics of this mask are beetled eyebrows, wide mouth, two horns, upward slanting eyes big ears, and a narrow face.

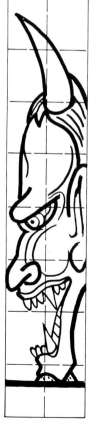

HOW TO CARVE

- The face is perpendicular to the stand.
- Photographs 1 -8 show the rough cuts, and photo 9 the separate sections.

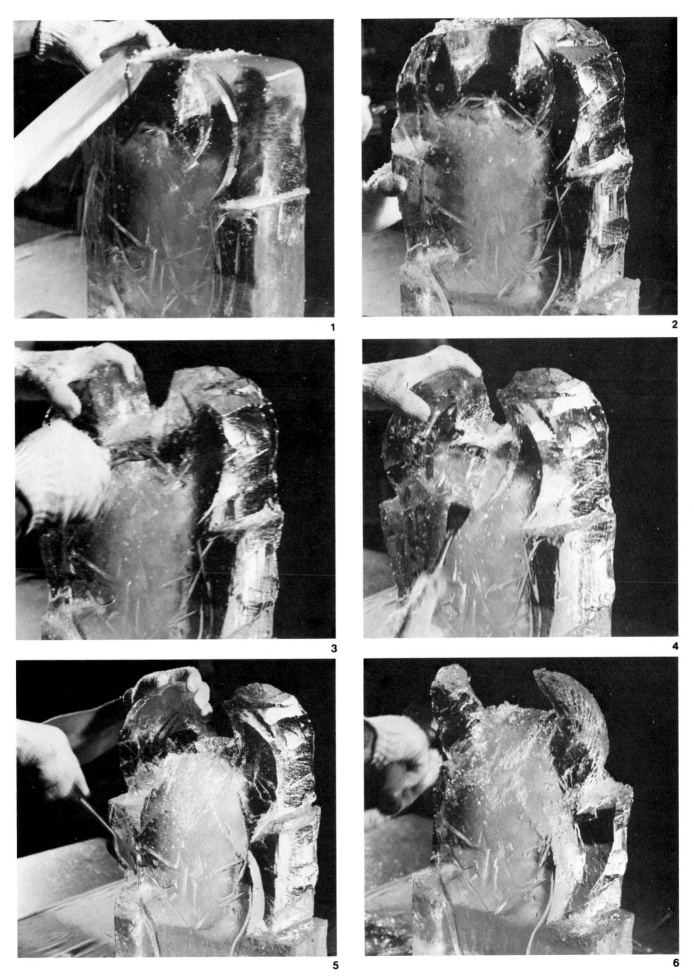

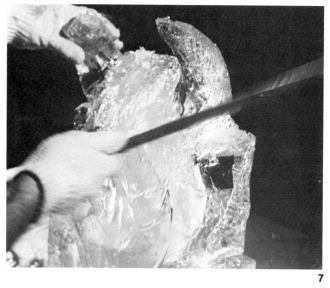

7

8

9

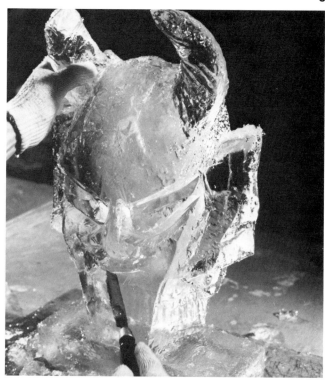

10

11

- On the face, all the separate details are exagerated (photos 9, 10, and 13-18).
- To do the mouth, start with a small circle, enlarge it to include the teeth, and then work upward from the nose, filling in the detail (photo 13).

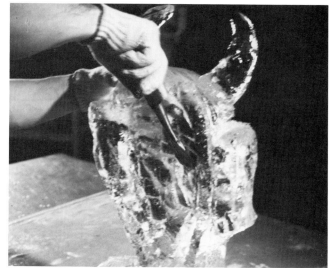

12

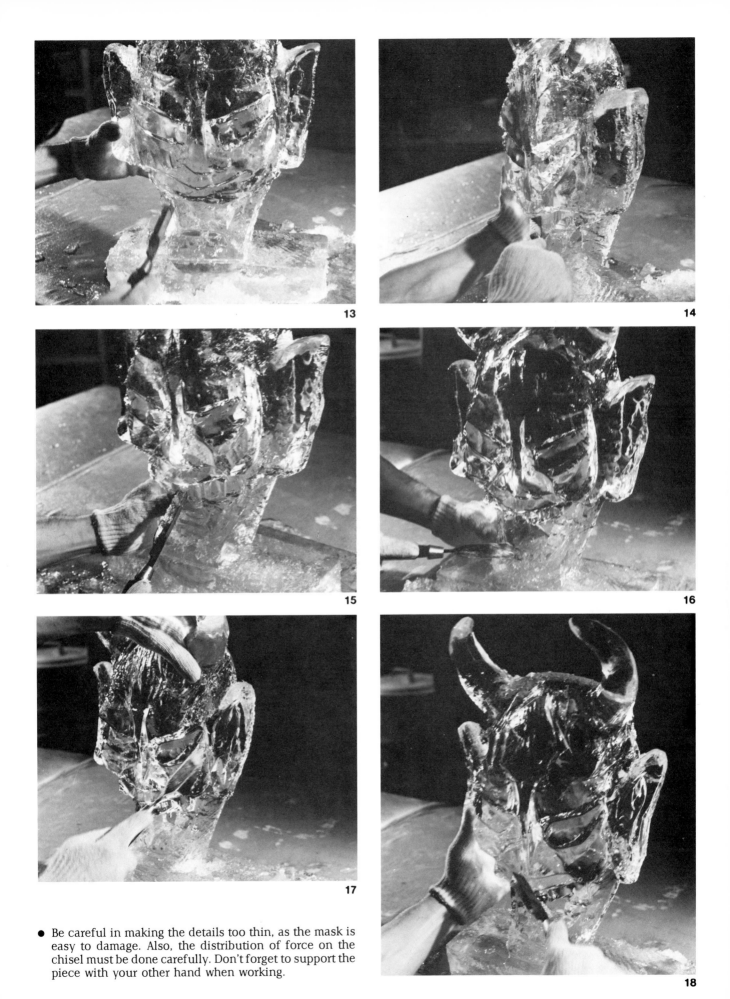

- Be careful in making the details too thin, as the mask is easy to damage. Also, the distribution of force on the chisel must be done carefully. Don't forget to support the piece with your other hand when working.

13

14

15

16

17

18

7 小鳥と巣

SMALL BIRDS AND NEST

Ice 1/6 A Cut

There are two small birds on the edge of the nest. This represents the birds either sitting on their eggs or gathering food. In this piece, the wings and necks of the two birds are different. They perch on the nest at different angles.

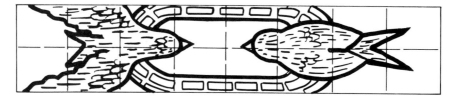

1

3

HOW TO CARVE
- The two birds are balanced to each other as well as to the figure as a whole, and should be finished together (photos 1-9)

2

4

5

6

7

● It is vital to carve the thin parts with great care. The angle of the wings, the shape of the shoulders, and so on must be carefully done (photos 10-13).

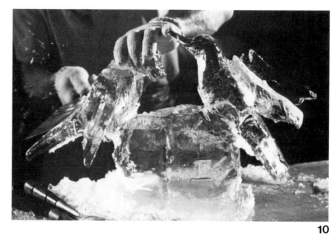

10

8

● Where there are extremely delicate shapes, the ice damages easily, so support the work and distribute pressure on the chisel evenly.

11

12

9

13

⑧ 二羽の小鳥

TWO BIRDS

Ice ¼ A Cut

This represents a peaceful nature scene of trees with singing birds on limbs. The two birds form an overall symetry, together with the tree limbs on which they are perched.

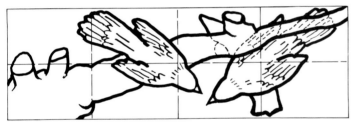

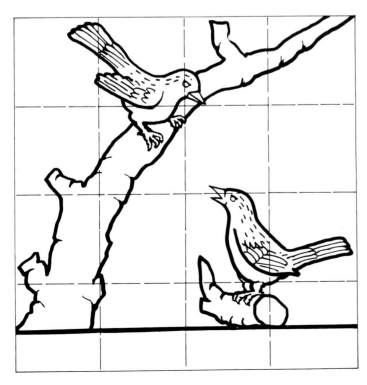

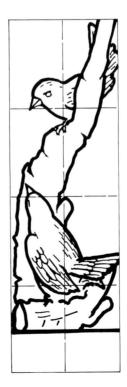

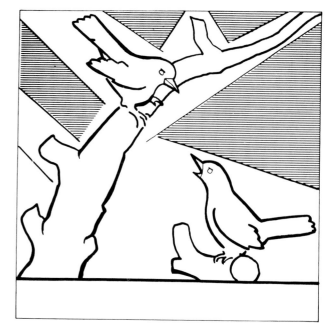

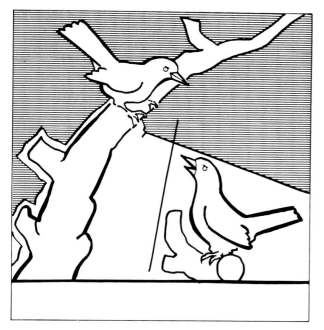

1

2

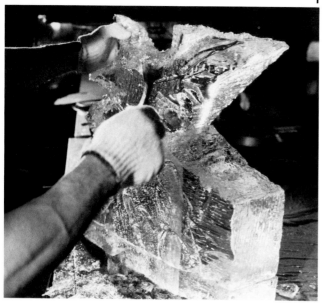

3

4

HOW TO CARVE

● The two birds are separate, and the rough etching must be accurate, or there will be errors in carving if the final drawings are not referred to frequently.

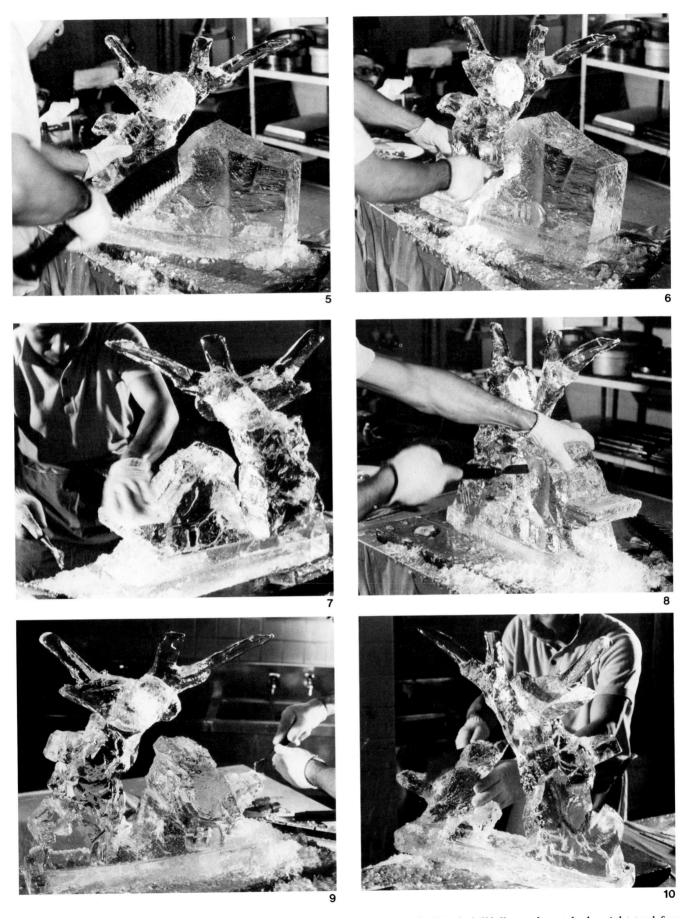

5

6

7

8

9

10

● There is a lot of waste ice, and care must be exercised or damage will result. Refer to the preceeding piece, "Small Birds and Nest."

● Use each chisel skillfully, and match the right tool for each particular operation. Remember to support the opposite side of the piece on which you are working.

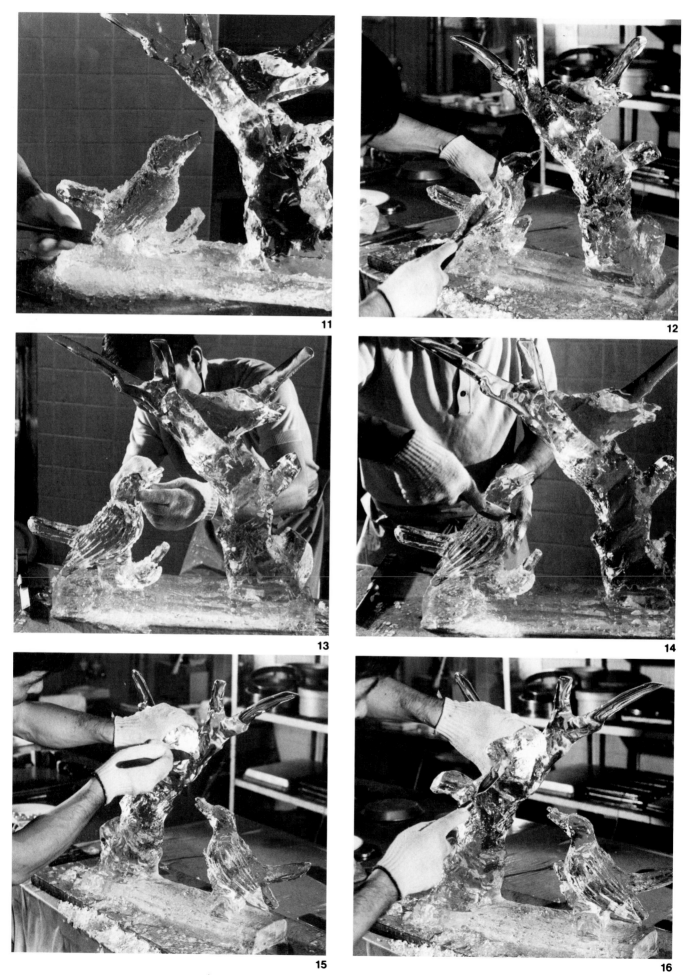

11

12

13

14

15

16

⑨ にわとり

9. ROOSTER

Ice ½ A Cut

A chicken is not extraordinary but, with a large crest and long tail, the male is quite beautiful.

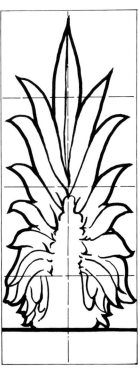

1　　2

3　　4

5　　6

HOW TO CARVE
● Of all the kinds of birds, this represents one with a plump, sleek, body. It is this kind of image that is important.

● The lines of the feathers are made with the angle chisel. However, if the lines are too regular, the piece will look strained and unnatural. Therefore, it is better to carve them in long, irregular strokes.

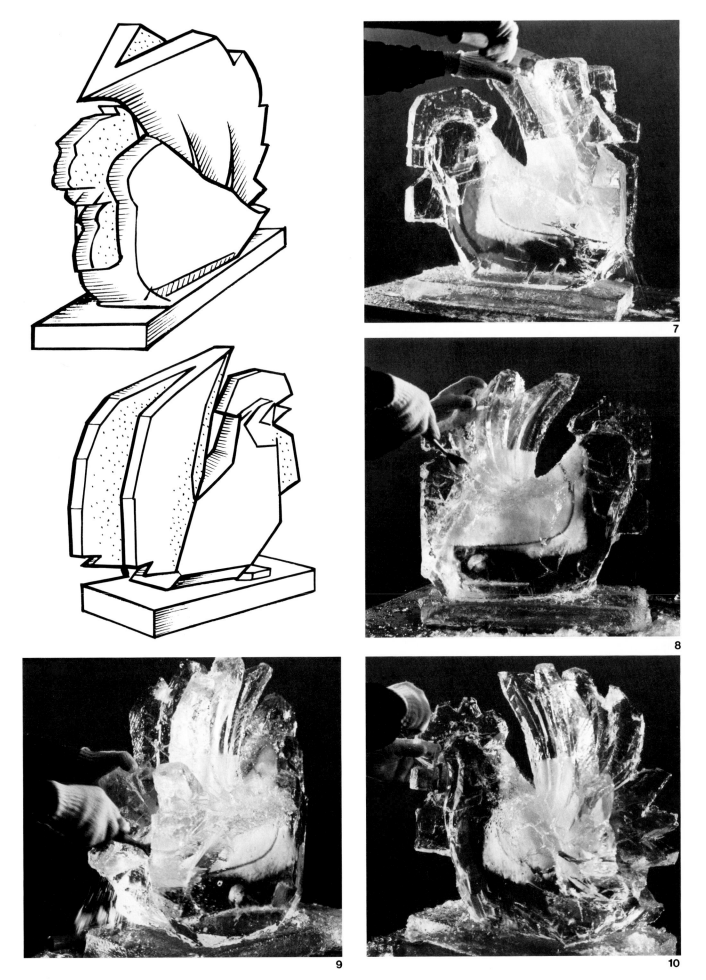

7

8

9

10

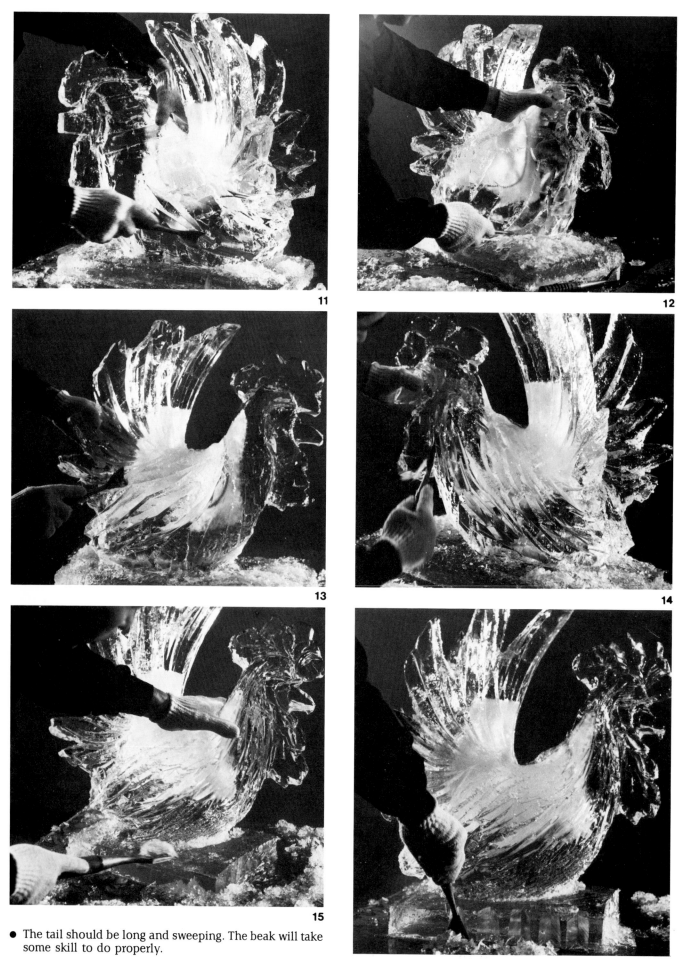

11

12

13

14

15

• The tail should be long and sweeping. The beak will take some skill to do properly.

16

10 伊勢えび

LOBSTER

Ice 1/6 A Cut

A dark-red lobster radiates beautiful form amd color. This carving brings these qualities out. The body is flat and long, the tail curves under, and the head curves forward, so the piece is balanced and stable.

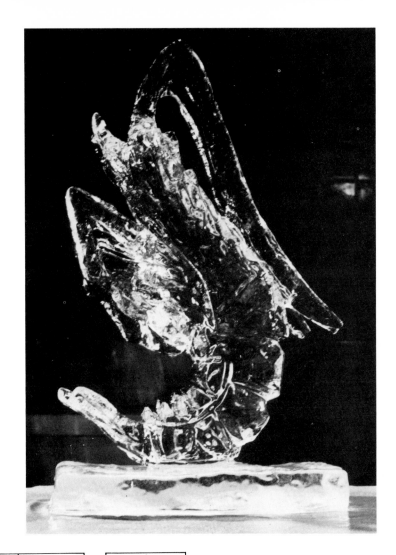

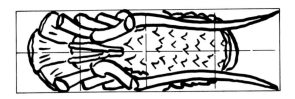

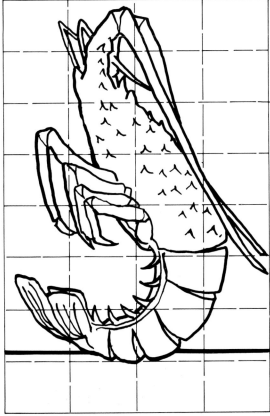

1

2

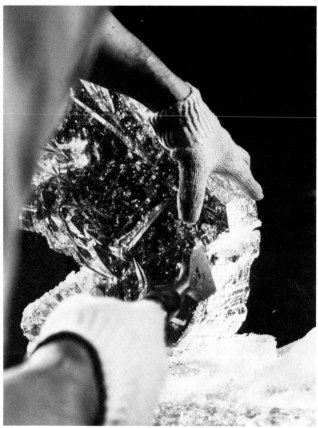

3

4

HOW TO CARVE

- Cut out the rough shape of the body and legs (photos 1-10).
- Emphasize the joints, tail plates, long antenna, and body armor.

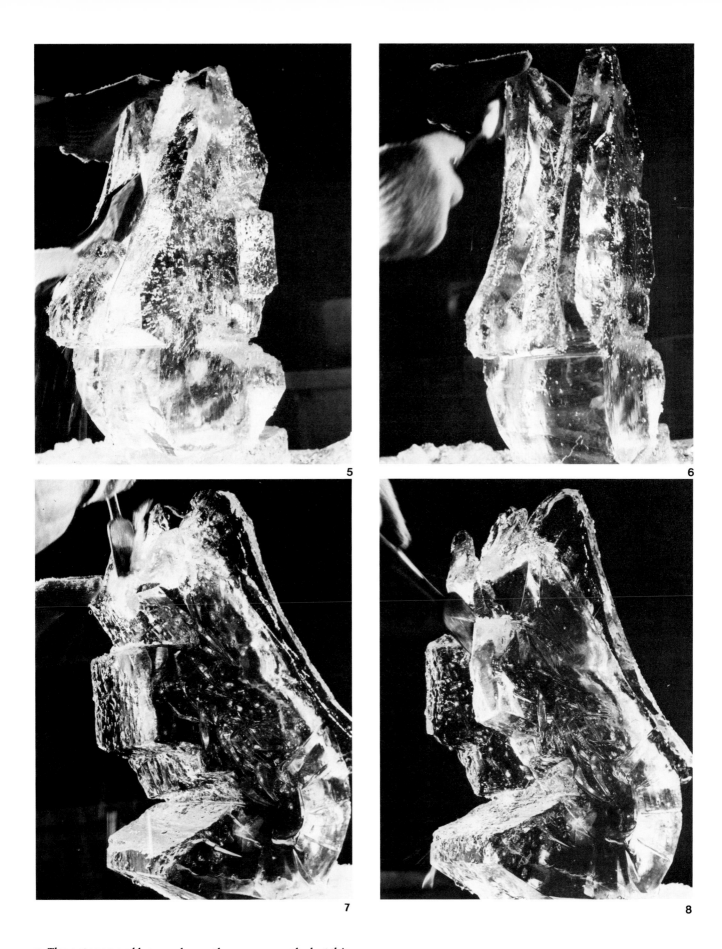

5

6

7

8

- The antenna and legs are larger than proper scale, but this gives the piece the desired unusual feeling (photos 11-16).
- The back shell is done, then the face, legs, and antenna.

- Do the antenna last. Do not use unreasonable force; work slowly and carefully.

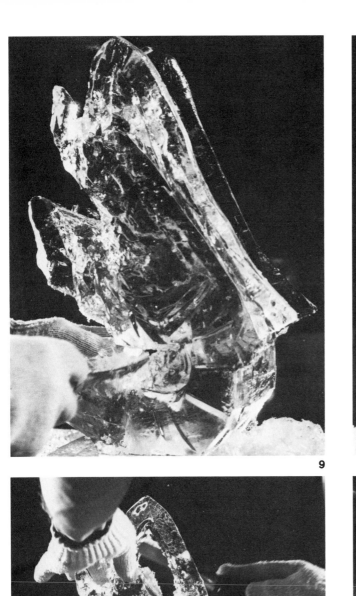

9

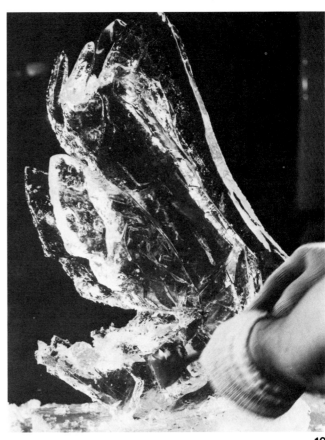

10

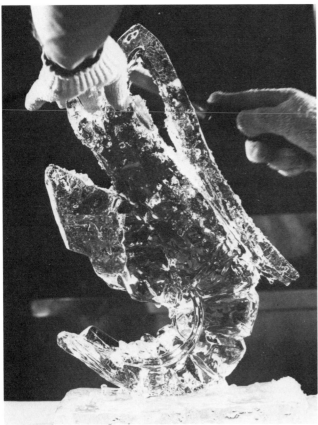

11

12

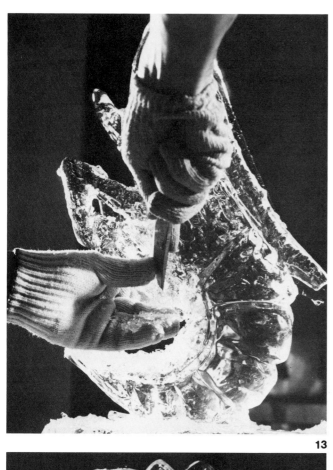

13

14

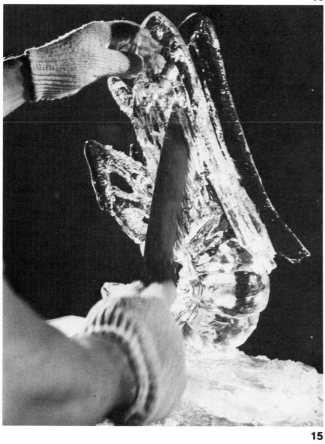

15

16

11 ぶどうの器

11. BASKET WITH GRAPES

Ice ⅓ Cut

For a fringe, this woven basket has bunches of grapes hanging at both ends. If you wish to use this basket for displaying wine, the length of the bottle of wine will be the determining factor of how long the basket should be.

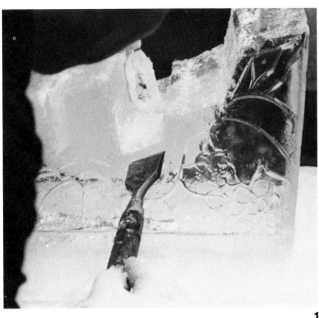

1

2

HOW TO CARVE

● When making this container, refer back to the "Basket with Wings," or to the "Basket with Ribbon"

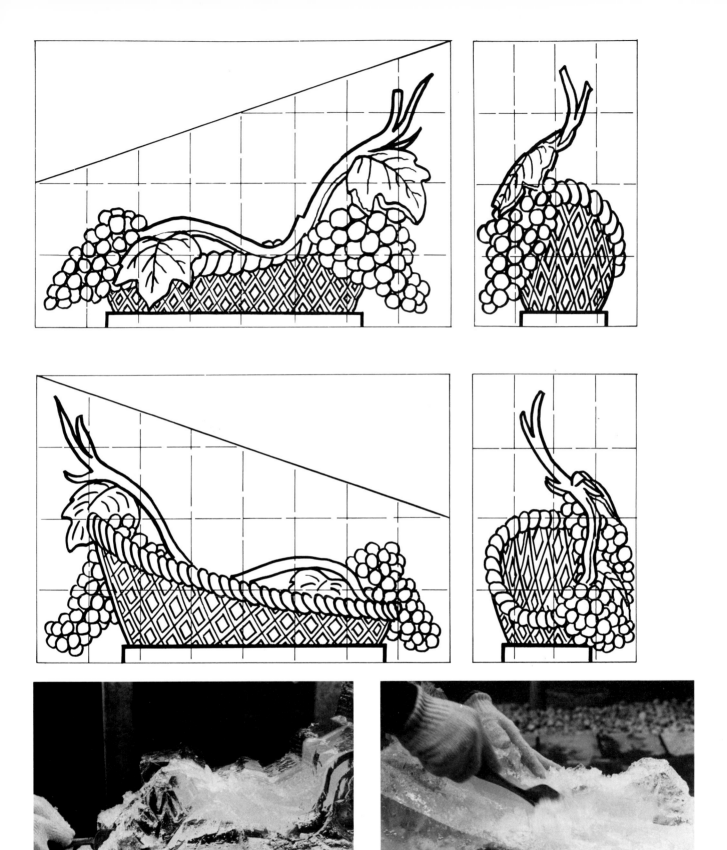

3

4

● To begin, cut out the oval shape and roughly cut out the inside (photos 1-7).

● Next, do the fringe of grapes, then the grape vine (photos 8-10).

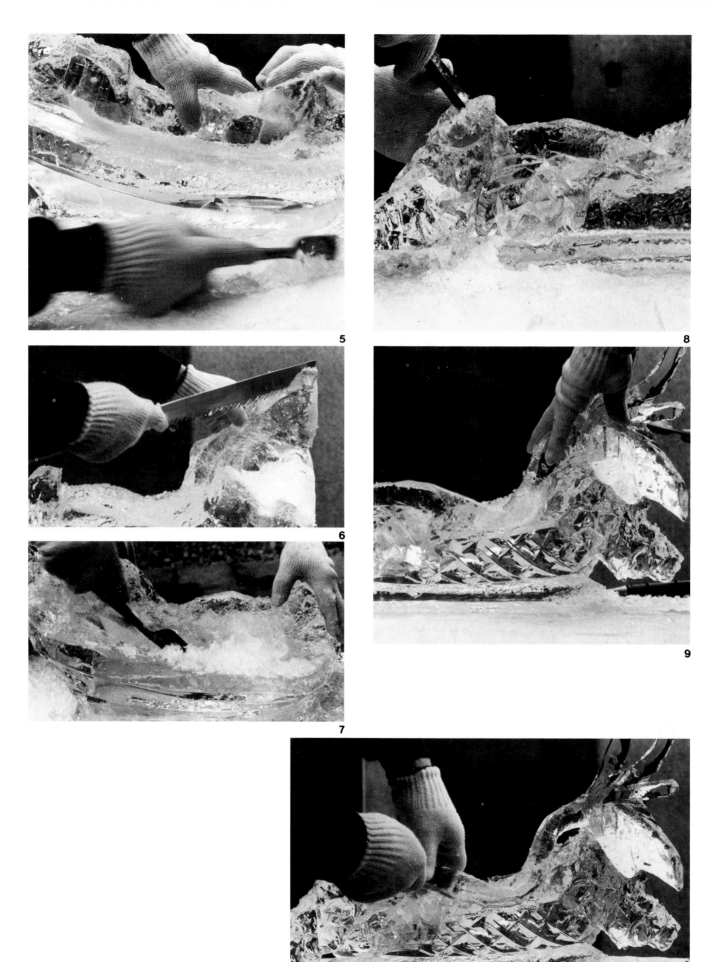

5

8

6

9

7

● The last step is finishing the basket itself.

10

12 ぶどうの飾り

GRAPES IN A RING

Ice ¼ A Cut

In this difficult exercise, there is a grapvine entwined about a ring. It is necessary to be careful in sculpturing the grapevine, and to fully understand the composition of the piece.

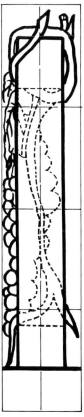

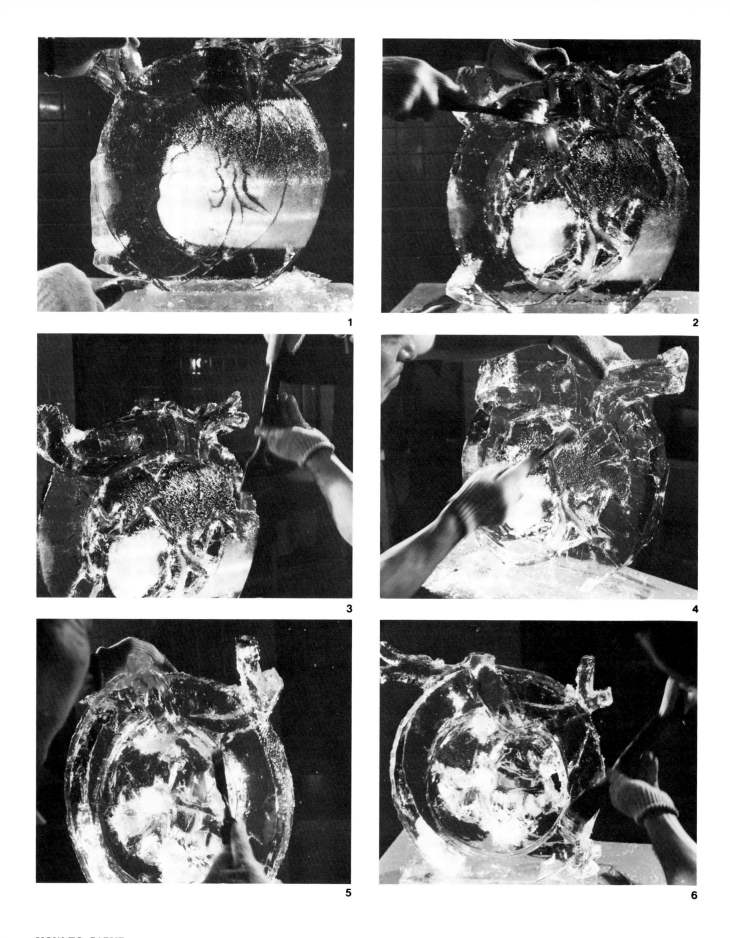

1

2

3

4

5

6

HOW TO CARVE
- Develop the outline of the stem outside of the ring, then roughly do the thickness of the ring, and then the stem.
- Cut out the unused ice within the ring, and widen the inside to its proper size (photos 1-12).
- As the piece nears completion, it is easy to damage. Cut

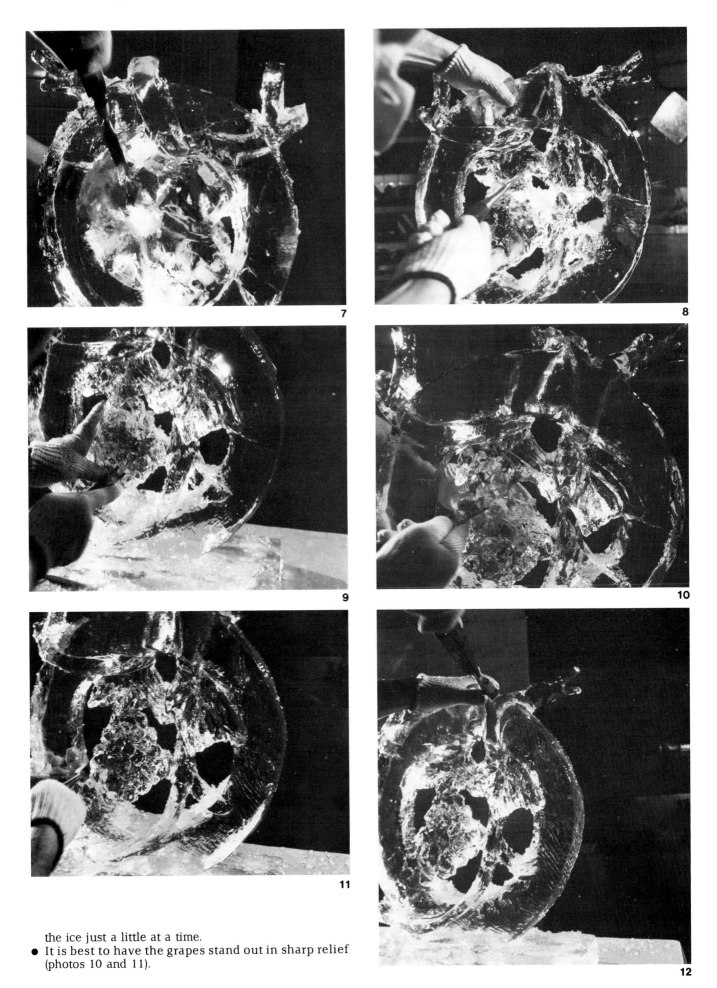

the ice just a little at a time.
● It is best to have the grapes stand out in sharp relief (photos 10 and 11).

13 御所車

OX CARRIAGE

Ice ½ A Cut

This ox carriage was used by the nobility of ancient Japan for ceremonies. You should refer back to the many points it holds in common with the Japanese-style bucket, the five-story Pagoda, and other pieces. The carriage is supported on spoked wheels, and rests leaning forward on the shafts. The roof supports are at right angles to the carriage body, and the wheels are large.

HOW TO CARVE

● The main theme of the piece is to make clear-cut angles. Cut away the unused ice with the handsaw, then rough out the section of the roof posts. The length between the uprights is equal to the diameter of the wheels. The shafts are perpendicular to the roof posts, which are parallel to each other.

1

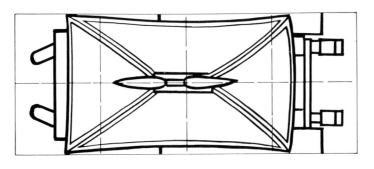

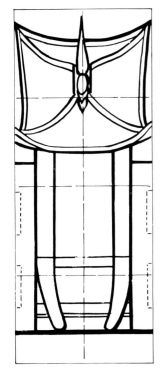

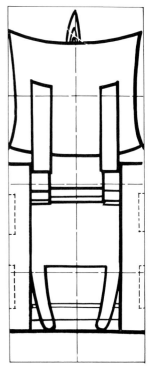

2

3

4

5

- Cut into the center of the carriage from both sides, determining the thickness of the roof posts (photos 10-13).
- Bring out the details of the entire carriage using the chisels.
- Be careful that everything, such as the roof posts, roof, and shafts, is symetrical.

6

7

14 鷹

HAWK

Ice ½ A Cut

The hawk, like the eagle, is a bird of prey, so their body shapes are similar. A hawk is smaller than an eagle, its feathers are dark brown, and it has a white crest on its belly. The wings are long, the beak is curved downward and the talons are quite sharp. This piece shows the hawk taking off after prey from a rock.

HOW TO CARVE
● First cut out the wings, then the tail, neck, head, feet and rock, in that order.
● Usually, one would proceed by etching the outline, cutting then finishing, but in this situation, the above steps should be followed.

1

2

3

4

5

6

7

8

● This takes an intermediate level of skill, but after doing the previous pieces, you should be able to do it. You should try.

9

10

11

12

● Refer to the "Eagle" exercise, and carve carefully.

15 楽　譜

SHEET MUSIC

Ice ½ B Cut

This piece was cut for a music class party, and can be said to have an unusual theme. The small birds are used as a device to indicate enjoyment of the music.

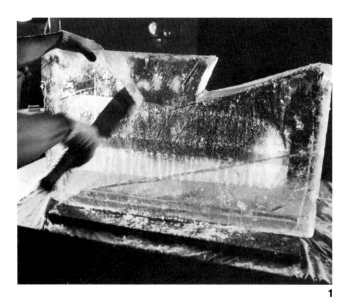

1

2

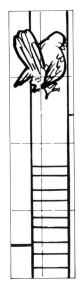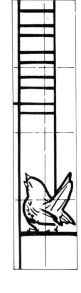

HOW TO CARVE

- There are five lines in the bar, so first cut out the bar then the five lines, and then the notes scattered across the bar. The lines penetrate through the ice (photos 1-6).

- The notes are cut slightly oval, but you should make them round at first.

4

3

5

6

7

8

9

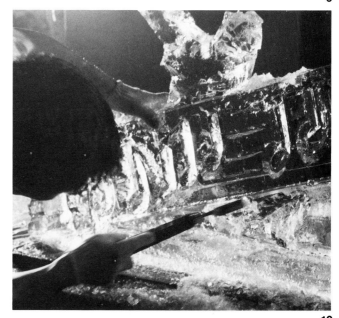

10

11

● The two birds are cut so that they face each other (photos 7-13).

12

13

14

15

16

● After the piece is roughly carved out, finish the birds first, then the music, then the stand (photos 14-16).

16 ばら-I

ROSE — I

Ice ½ C Cut

This rose has elegance in its artistic composition of petals and leaves. You should alter any aspects of this to evoke your own personal creativity.

1

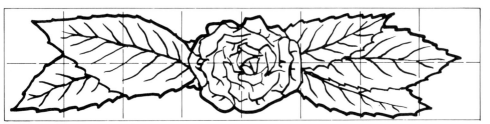
上面
Top view

前面
Front view

後面
Back view

2

3

4

5

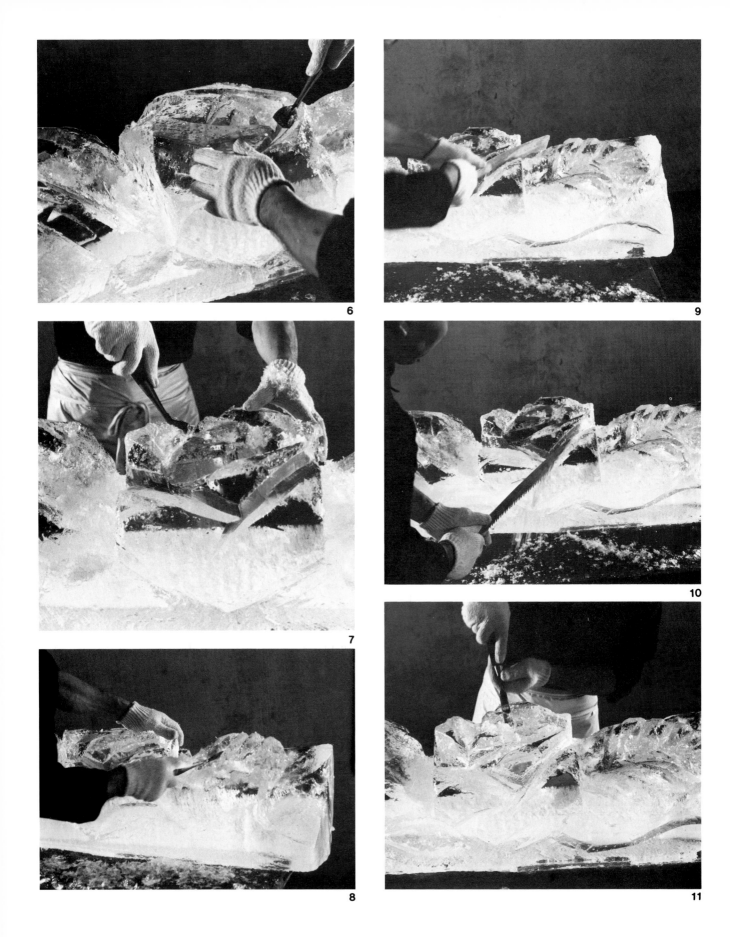

6

9

7

10

8

11

HOW TO CARVE

● There are five leaves pointing outward; all five are different.

● The rose itself is in the center and is started from a circle with the petals cut in varying patterns (photos 1-5, 12 and 13).

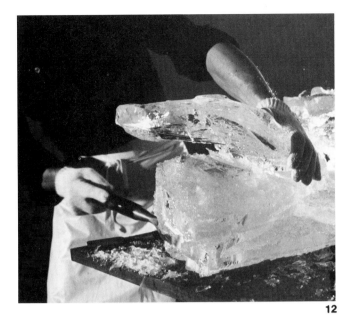

12

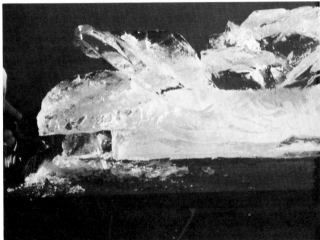

13

14

15

16

17

18

- You can use a saw on the petals, each of which should be slightly pointed (photos 6-11 and 14).
- Carve the leaves as beautifully as possible (photos 16-18).

17 ばら-II

ROSE — II

Ice ¼ A Cut

This is small, but very difficult. On the details,
use the flat chisel, the angle chisel and the saw
properly, at the right time and place.

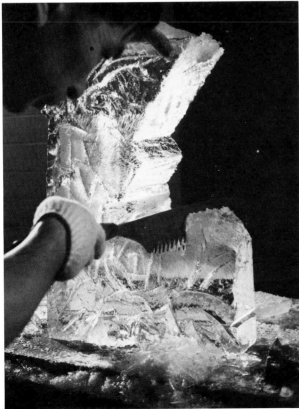

HOW TO CARVE
- The gaps between the stake and branch and between the flowers and leaves are carefully cut out (photos 1-11).
- While sculpting the flower and leaves, refer to "Rose–I."

1

3

4

5

6

● When cutting out the stake, be careful to balance it on
  both sides as well as from front to back. In finishing, use
  the chisel with care (photos 12-14).

7

8

9

10

● Use the angle chisel when making the stake and the rose bush branch.

11

12

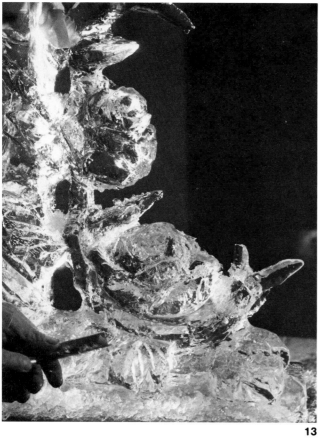

13

14

5 上級作品

ADVANCED PIECES

1 鷲

EAGLE

Ice 1 Piece

The figure of an eagle with out-stretched wings is a frequent theme for ice carving. Once the proper sequence of carving is learned, it is not too difficult. Balance is important to express the image of the eagle.

  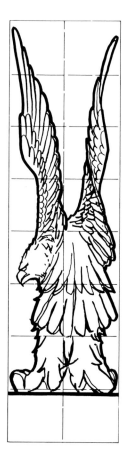

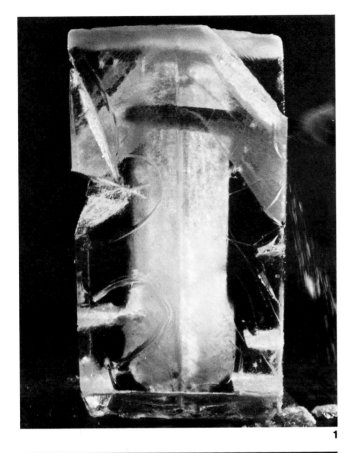

1

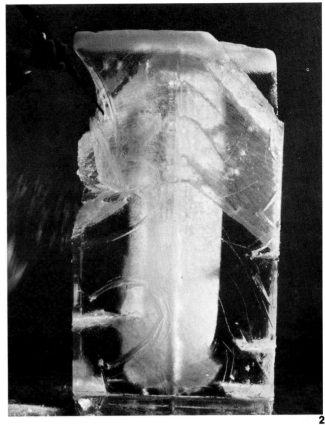

2

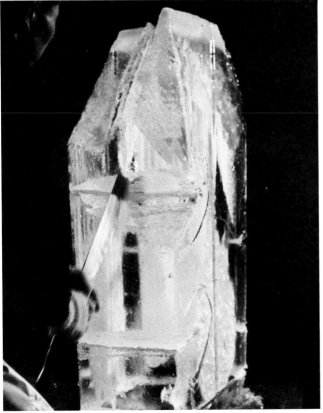

3

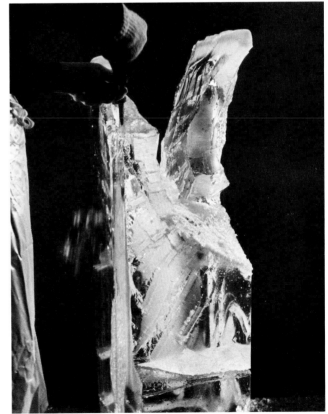

4

OBJECTIVES

- Etch the basic composition and cut it out with the saw, being careful not to cut too near the figure itself.
- Refering to the drawings, make the lines of the upward-

swept wings from head to tail.

- The eagle's beak is sharp. The whole head is about at the midpoint from the bottom on the front of the ice, with the tail a little lower.

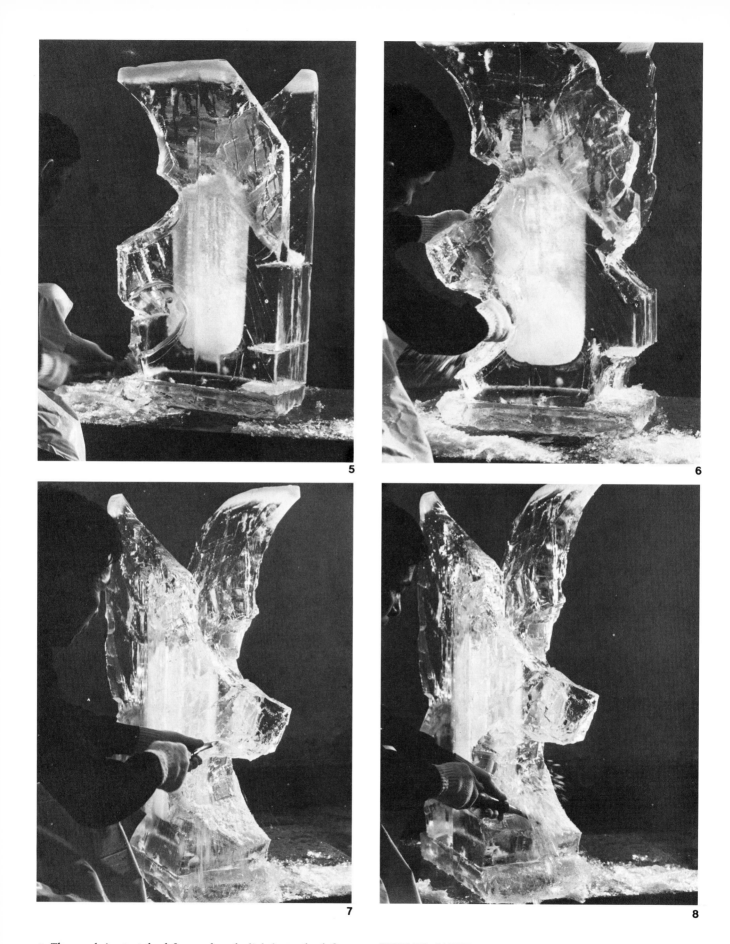

5

6

7

8

● The neck is stretched forward and slightly to the left.

HOW TO CARVE

(1) Cut away the unused areas of ice with the saw (photos 1 and 2).

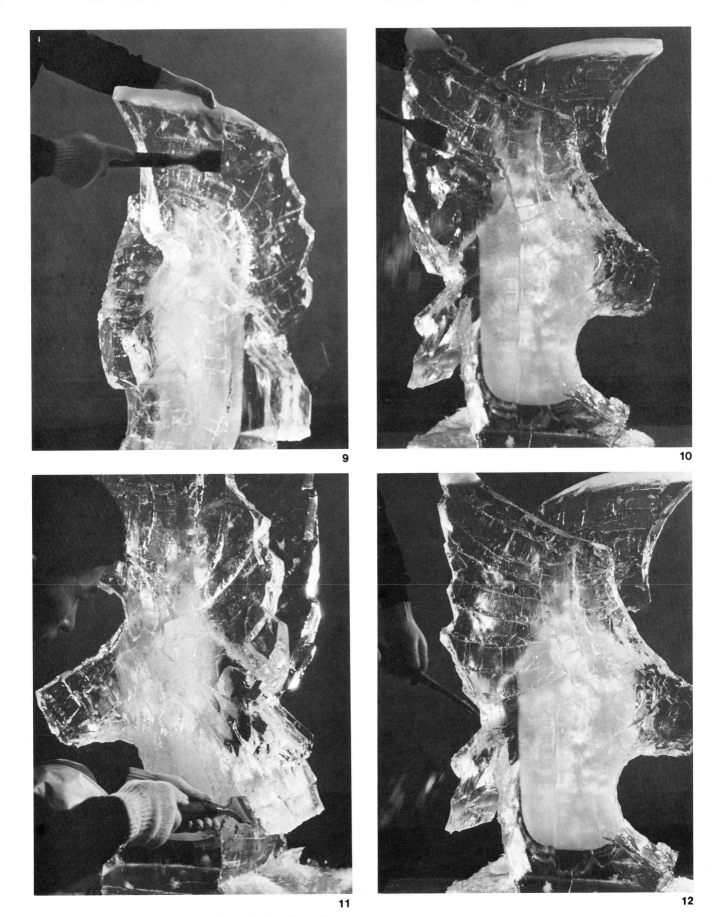

9

10

11

12

(2) Cut one wing angling farther forward than the other (photo 3).
(3) Cut away excess ice with a large flat chisel. Photo 4 shows the front view, cutting the curve of the wing from the inside. Photo 6 shows the final rough cut.
(4) Make the outline of the neck and legs, remembering to maintain the eagle's balance (photos 7 and 8).

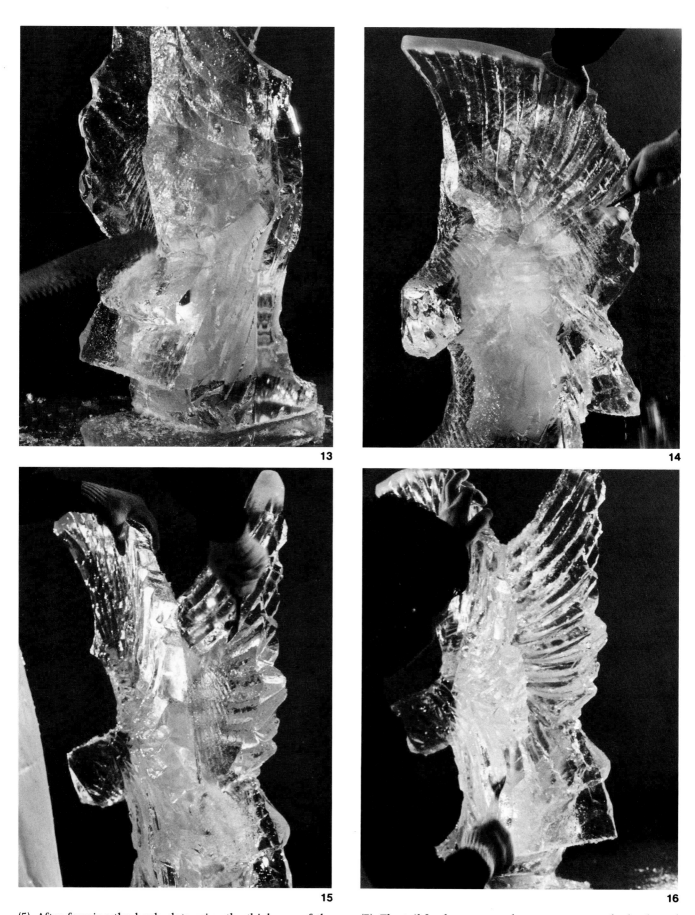

13

14

15

16

(5) After forming the back, determine the thickness of the wings (photo 9).

(6) Then do the other wing (photo 10).

(7) The tail feathers are on the same curve as the back, and are slanted downward (photos 11 and 12).

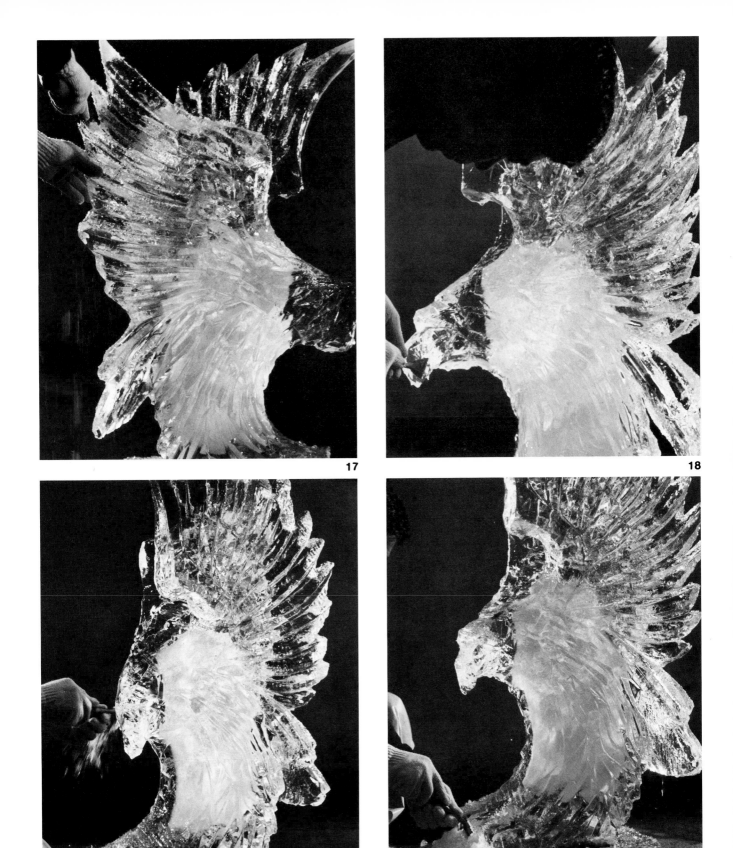

17

18

19

20

(8) Etch the lines of the feathers and of the wings with the angle chisel (photo 14).
(9) Do the same on the inside surface of the wings (photo 15).
(10) Etch the lines of the feathers on the tail, and finish up the detail on the wings (photos 16 and 17).
(11) The beak is the focal point of the eagle (photos 18 and 19).
(12) Finish the legs and talons (photo 20).

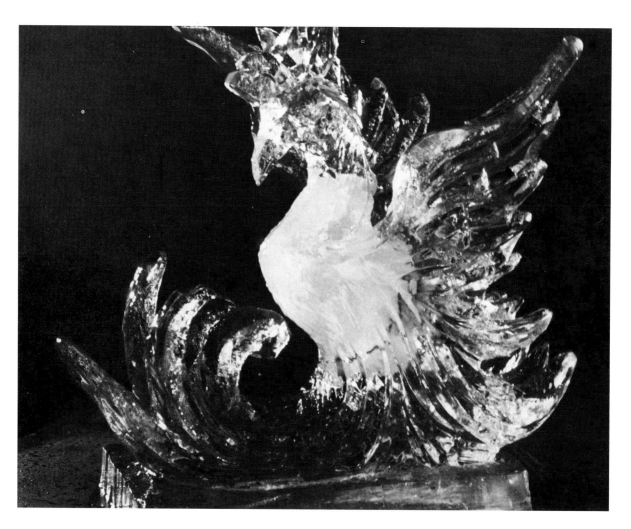

2鳳凰

2. PHOENIX

Ice 3/5 Cut

The phoenix was a mythical bird of ancient China. It was said to be a harbinger of good luck, like the dragon or the turtle. The bird usually looked as it was made of various different animals, but this one is of my creation.

HOW TO CARVE
● The full figure should be carved with care taken when carving the details.

1

2

3

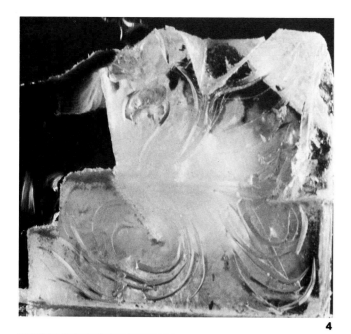

4

5

6

● Photos 1-10 show first the rough cuts, then the cut of the characteristic details. The open wings are cut slightly different from each other (photo 14).

7

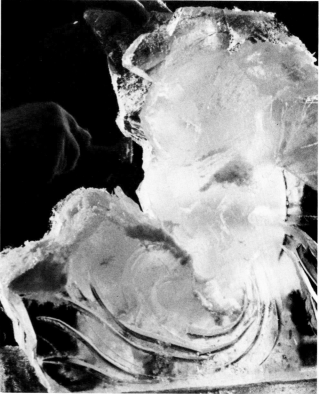

8

9

10

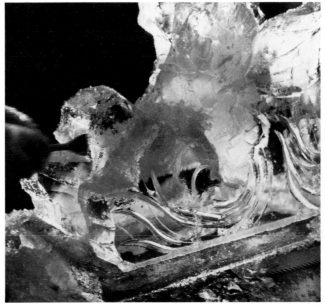

11

- The tail curls both backwards and forward; refer to the drawing to determine how to carve it. When carving the feathers, it is important to make one long continuous line (photos 15-19).

12

13

14

16

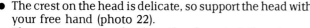

- The crest on the head is delicate, so support the head with your free hand (photo 22).
- The crest, wings, and tail are the characteristic points of the phoenix. Use the angle chisel when cutting these (photo 23).

17

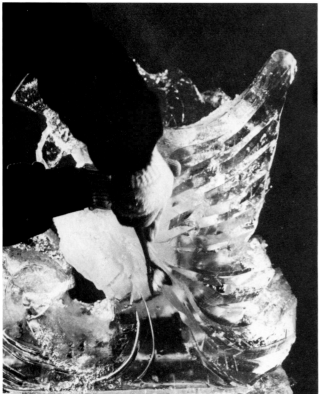

15

18

19

22

20

23

● Pay particular attention to the overall balanced effect of the wings and head.

21

③ スワン－I
SWAN — I

Ice 1 Piece

There are many different shapes in this beautiful swan; the long sloping neck, the wide wings, and a freedom-loving image are the themes.

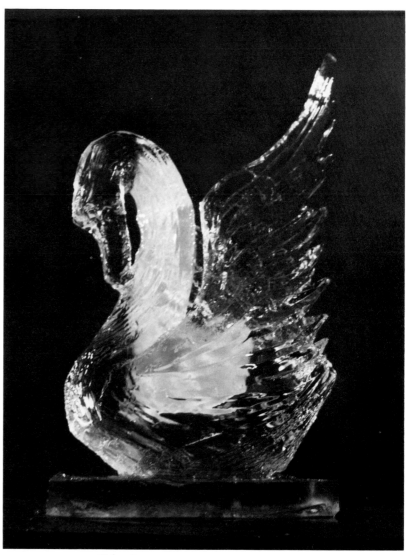

This shows the curve of the wing

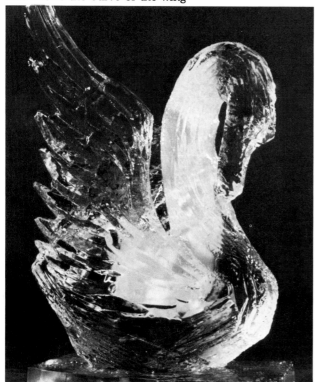

Side view

HOW TO CARVE

- When etching the plans, take note of the balance of the complete form, the size of the wings, and the proper angle of the neck.
- Refer to photos 1-3 when cutting away excess ice.

1

2

3

6

4

- Be very careful in maintaining balance when cutting the neck and body.
- When cutting out the shape, determine first the width of the wings, then the angle (photos 1-13).

5

7

8

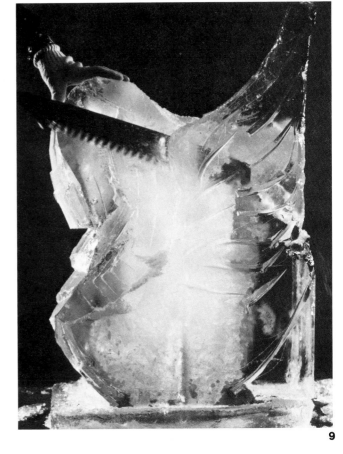

9

- It is important to cut the curve of the shoulder to the wing tip accurately.
- Cut out the details of the neck, head, and beak (photos 14-20).

10

11

12

13

- Not only is the neck long, but it is gently sloped (photo 18).
- Develop a soft effect for the whole piece.

14

15

16

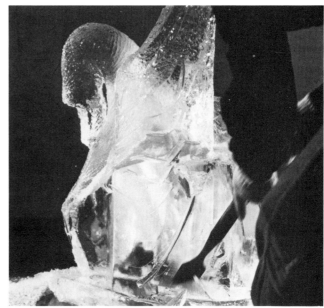

17

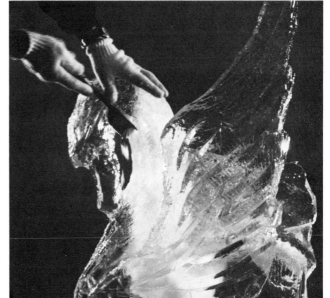

18

19

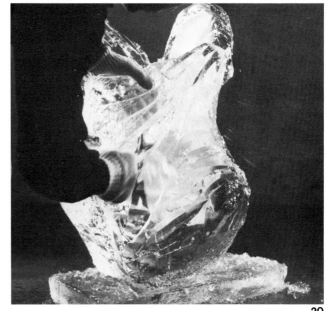

20

4 スワン－Ⅱ
SWAN — Ⅱ

Ice 1 Piece

Although the appearances of this swan differs from that of "Swan — Ⅰ", the techniques of carving are similar.

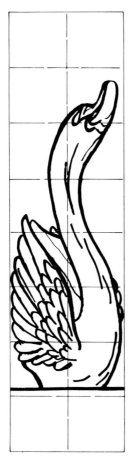

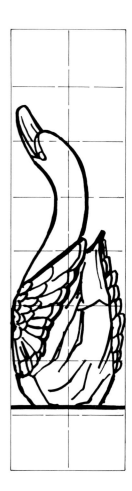

1

2

3

4

HOW TO CARVE
- Be careful when using the flat chisel to rough cut the neck. The lines should flow. This has a large influence on the overall appearance (photos 1-6).

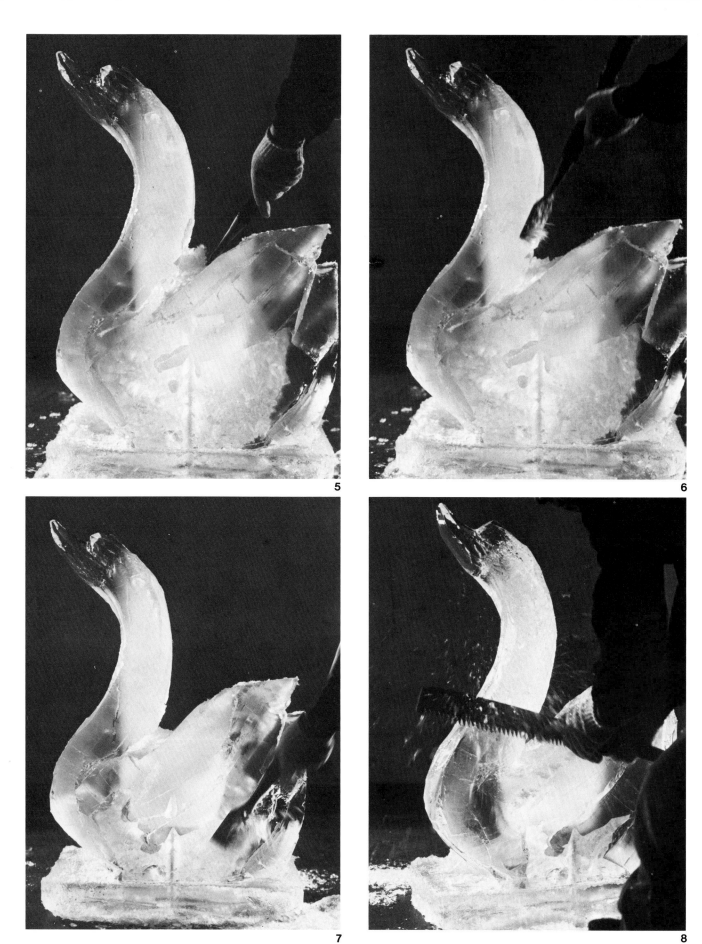

5

6

7

8

● The tail curves upward (photos 4, 7, and 9-11). Using the angle chisel, make smooth, upward-curving lines on the

9

10

11

12

wings (photos 10 and 11).
- When cutting the bill, support the neck (photo 12).

5 輪の上の スワン

SWAN ON A RING

Ice 1 Piece

The swan itself is symetrical; therefore, it is important to balance it on the ring, which is the stand. You can put flowers inside the ring and use it for a center decoration at a children's party, as I think that the whole harmonizes quite well.

The proportion of the swan to the ring is about 3/4; the ring diameter is the width of the ice. The swan is at a slight angle, with the wings pointing up.

1

2

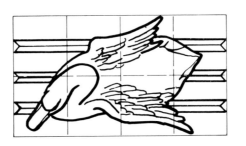

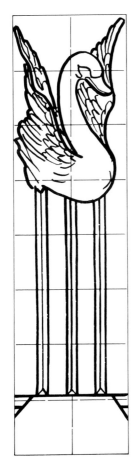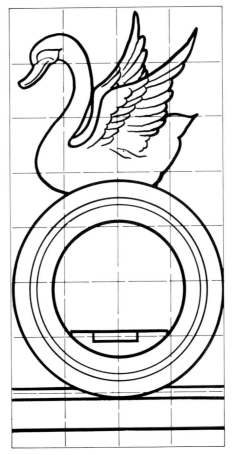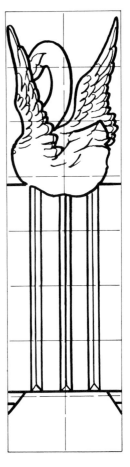

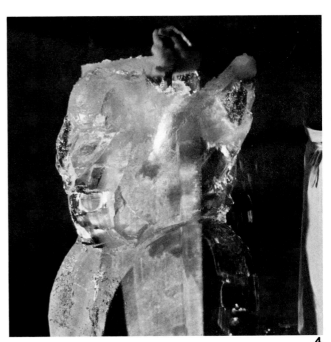

3

4

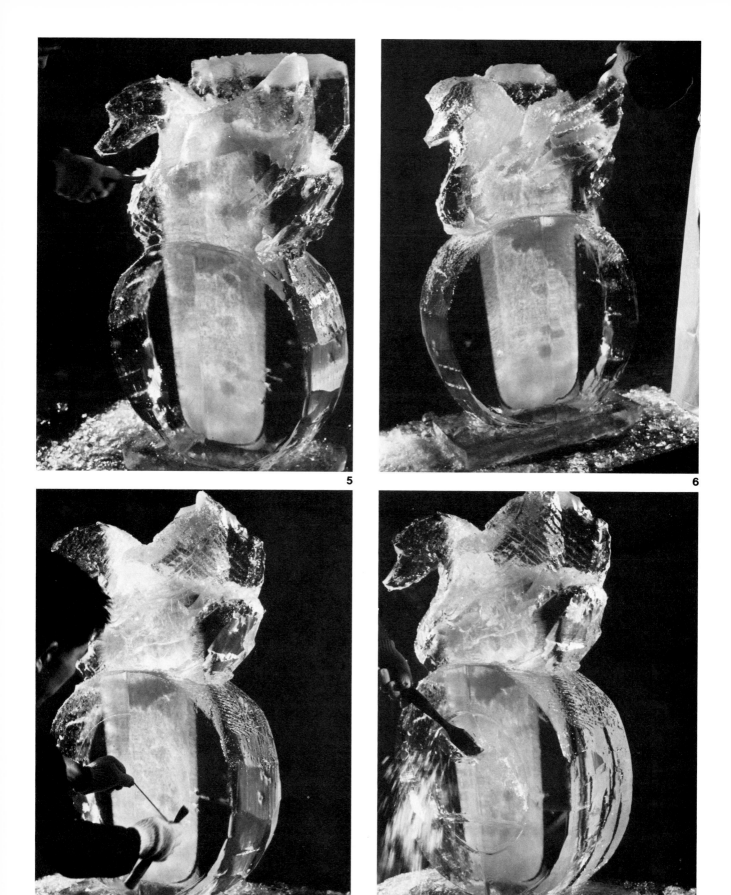

5

6

7

8

HOW TO CARVE
- First, etch the outside circle and then the swan on the ice, then cut them out (photos 1-6).

- Make a smaller concentric circle, and then cut this out (photos 7-16).

172

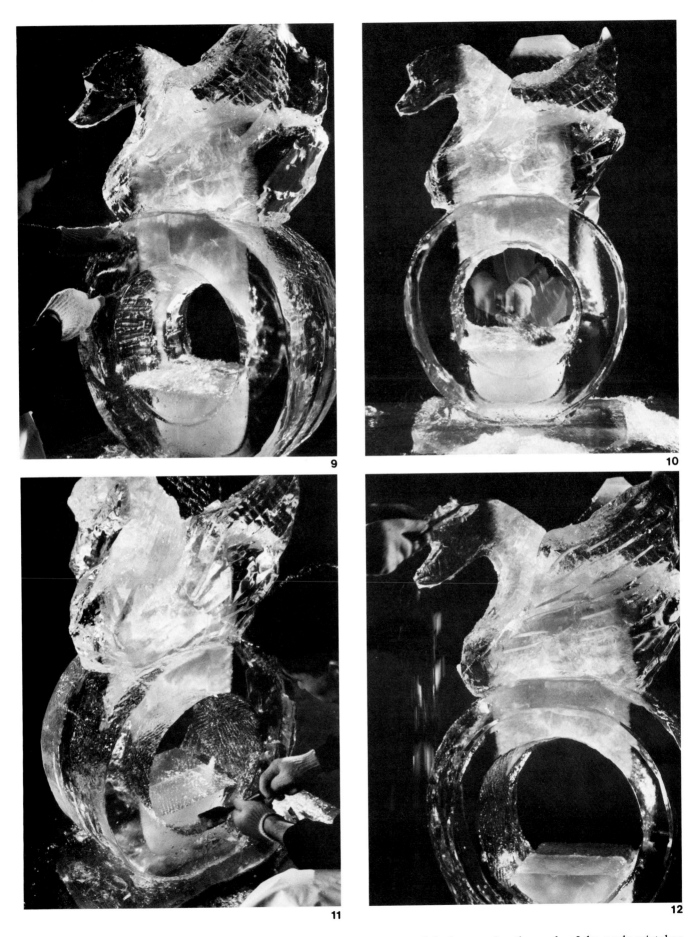

9

10

11

12

● Sculpt out the swan working from head to tail, using the saw.

● Be careful when cutting the angle of the neck; mistakes are easy.

13

14

15

16

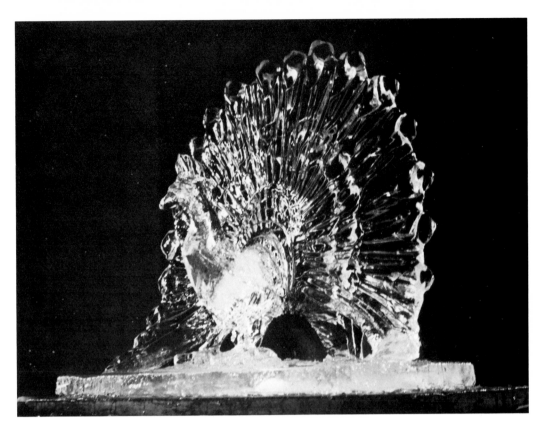

 PEACOCK   Ice 1 Piece

The peacock is a member of the pheasant family. The fascinating colors of the tail are very beautiful. Regretfully, one cannot show the colors, but one can show the fan-like tail to advantage. There is an impression of movement with the head at an angle.

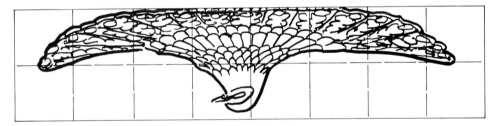

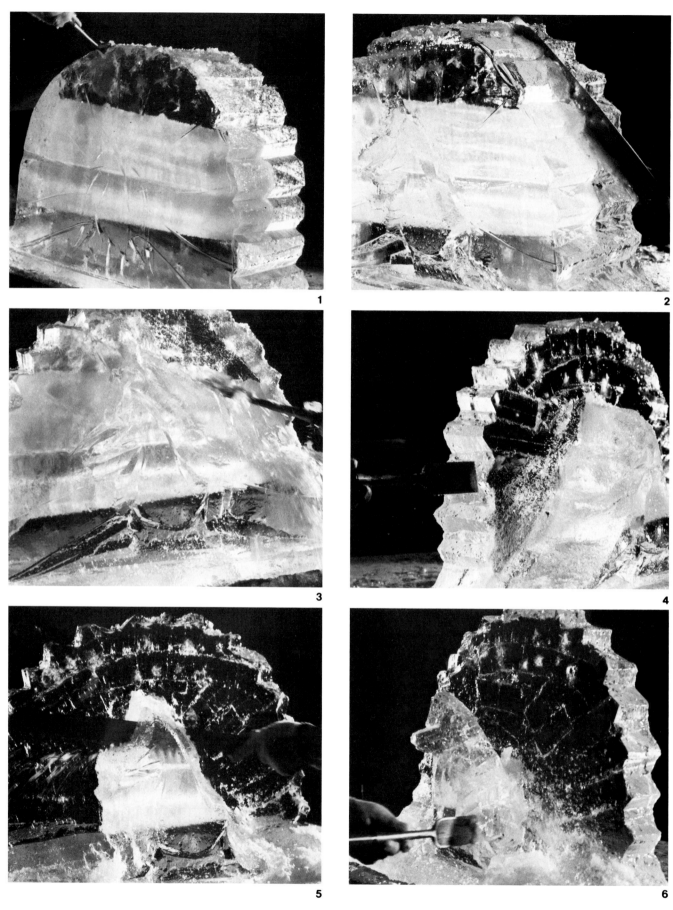

1
2
3
4
5
6

HOW TO CARVE

● In doing the details, I hope you use the right chisel on the large amount of detail work; for example, the angle chisel for cutting the circumference of the wings, the flat chisel for cutting the head and body, and the saw to make the thickness of the wings uniform (photos 1-12).

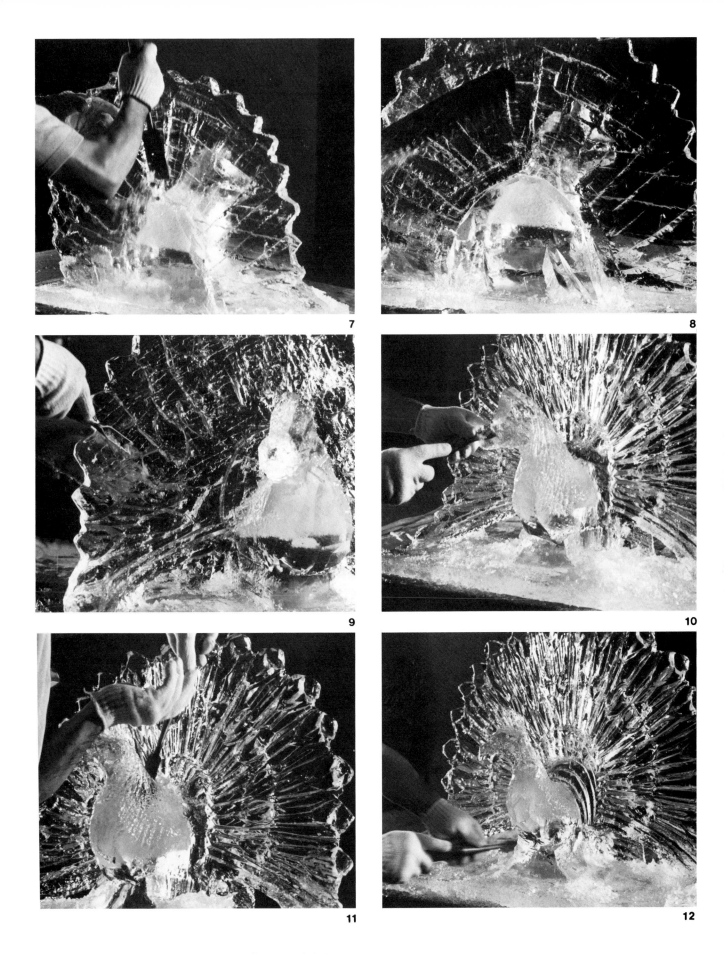

- The wide tail is fairly thin and easy to damage while being cut. If the cuts are too shallow, the effect will be reduced.

7 尾長鳥

LONG-TAILED COCK

Ice 1 Piece

The long-tailed cock is native to Japan, but is relatively rare. The tail is said to grow about 3 meters long. In this exercise, the long-tailed male stands on a high perch, with a female standing on a lower perch to emphasize the tail. This gives balance, and makes the comparison of the two birds easy.

1

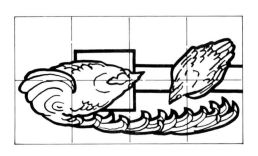

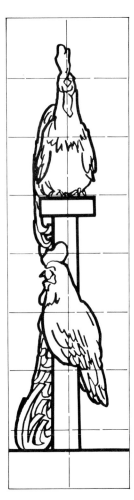

2

3

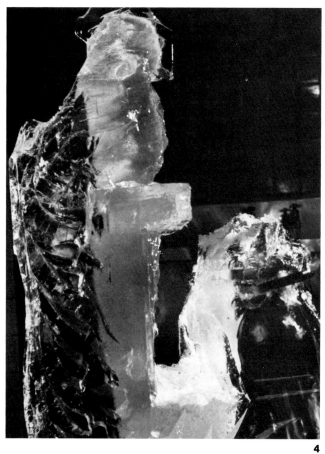

4

5

6

7

HOW TO CARVE
- Excluding the tail, the technique for carving the long-tailed cock is the same as that for the rooster.

- When carving the tail, work from both sides, curving in towards the center and down towards the tip (photos 1-7 and 11).

180

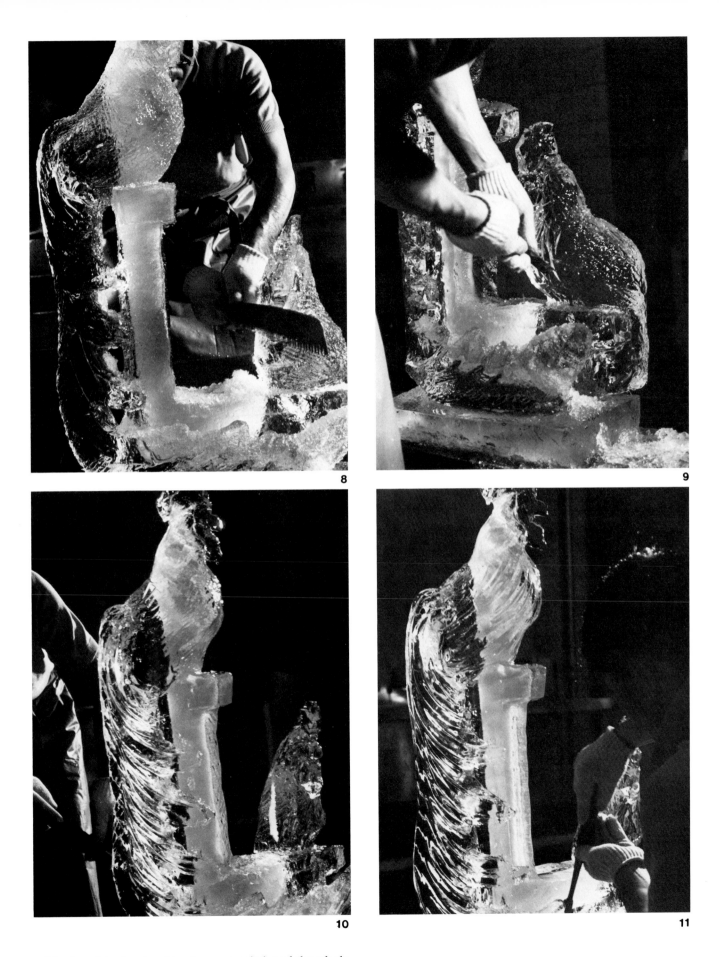

8

9

10

11

● The female's chest and back are rounded, and the whole
body is plump and full (photos 8 and 9).

 鶴

CRANE

Ice 1 Piece

A crane standing in the marsh is an elegant figure with a long neck, head and legs. This is the feeling you should try to portray. The characteristic long, thin legs are difficult and do not fully support the crane.

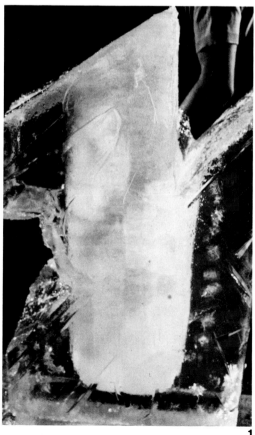

1

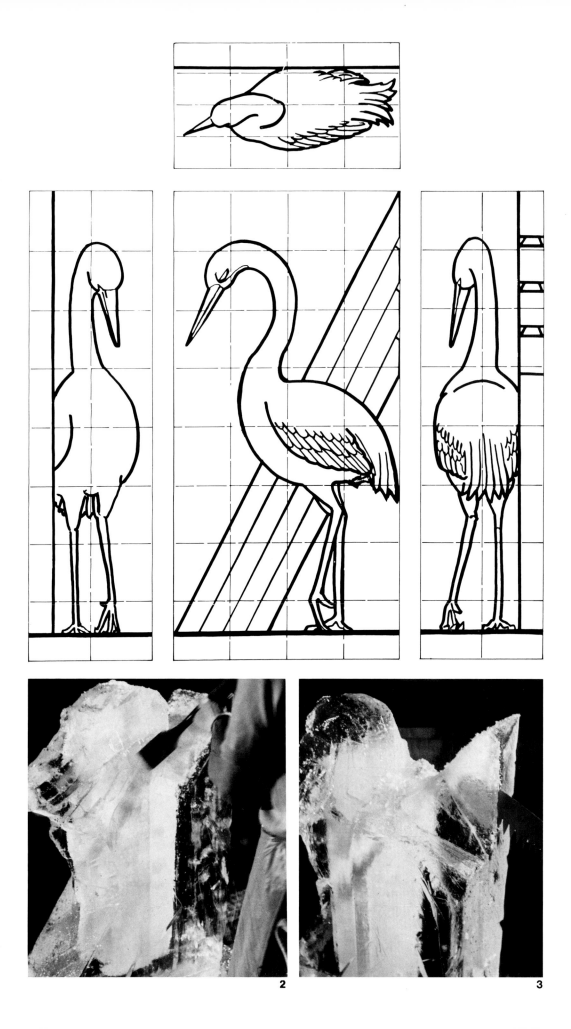

2

3

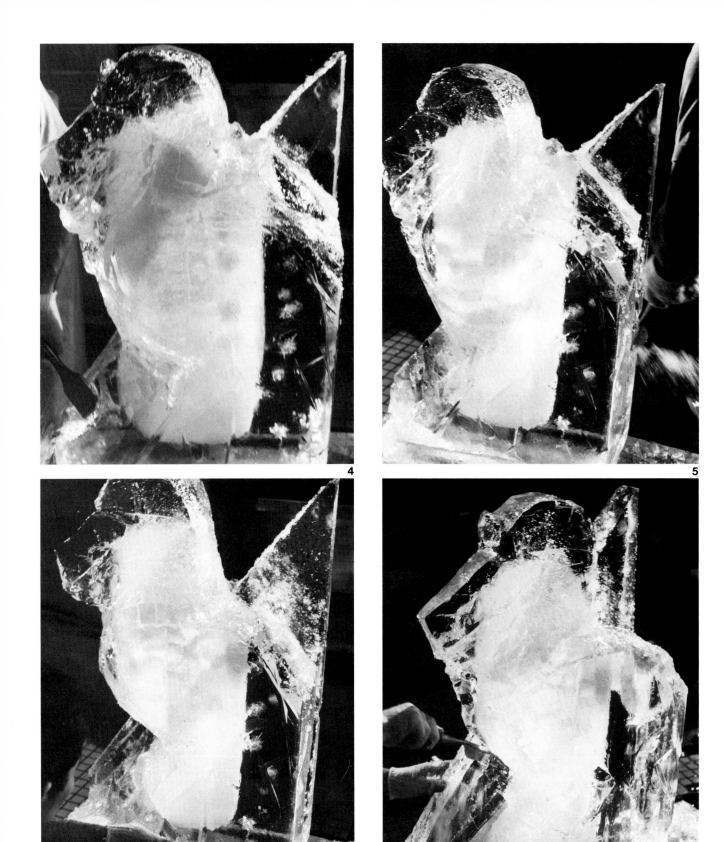

4

5

6

7

HOW TO CARVE
- Balance is vital in the form of the crane, so keep this in mind when carving.
- It is very important that the neck is done carefully, slightly tapering towards the head.
- Finish the thin legs and bill last, carving gently to avoid breakage.

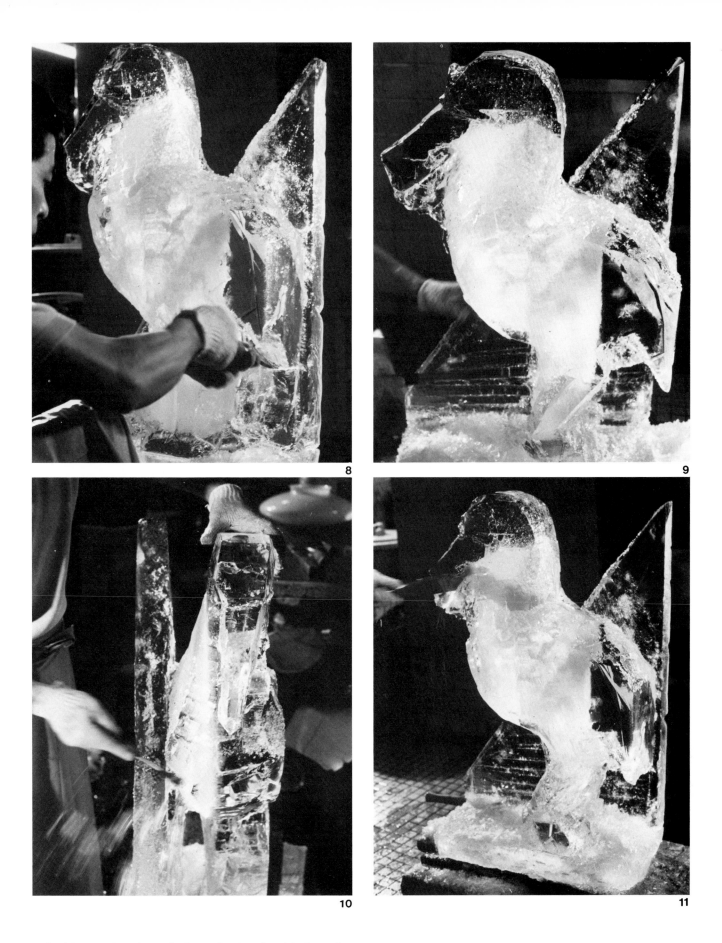

8

9

10

11

● In this exercise, the technique of using the chisel to take
off small shavings must be mastered, as the thin pieces
break easily (photos 1-15).

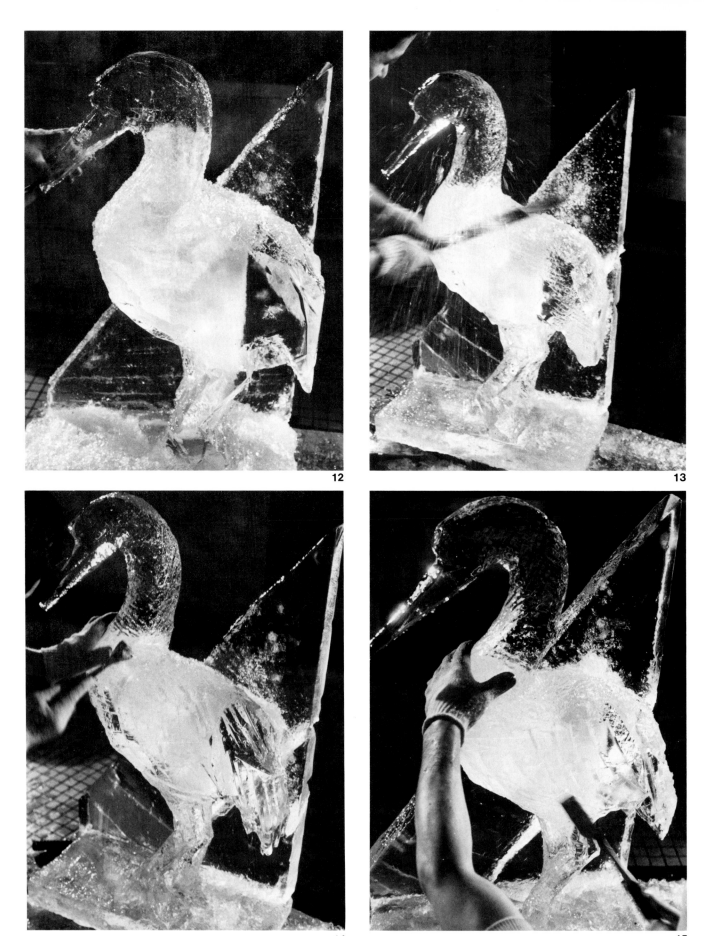

12

13

14

15

● The characteristic bill is long and narrow (photos 11 and 12).

16

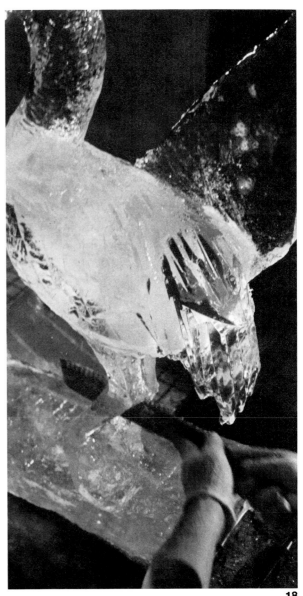

18

17

⑨ エンゼル フィッシュ

ANGEL FISH

Ice 1 Piece

The beautiful angel fish is about the same level of difficulty as the swan and the eagle. The basic figure is rather simple, but becomes complex when carved against a background of seaweed. Thus, it is important to compose the whole carving so it appears that both the fish and the seaweed are moving. To make it three dimensional, the body of the fish is separated from the seaweed; the tail, dorsal and pectoral fins are connected to the seaweed.

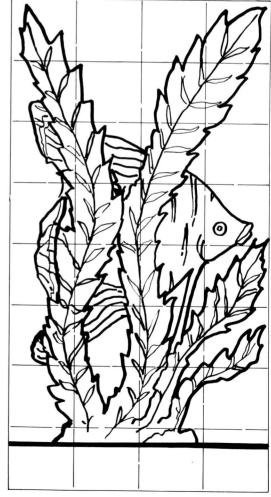

1

2

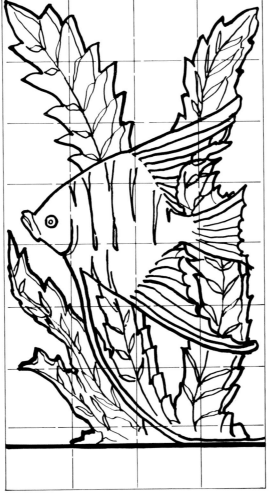

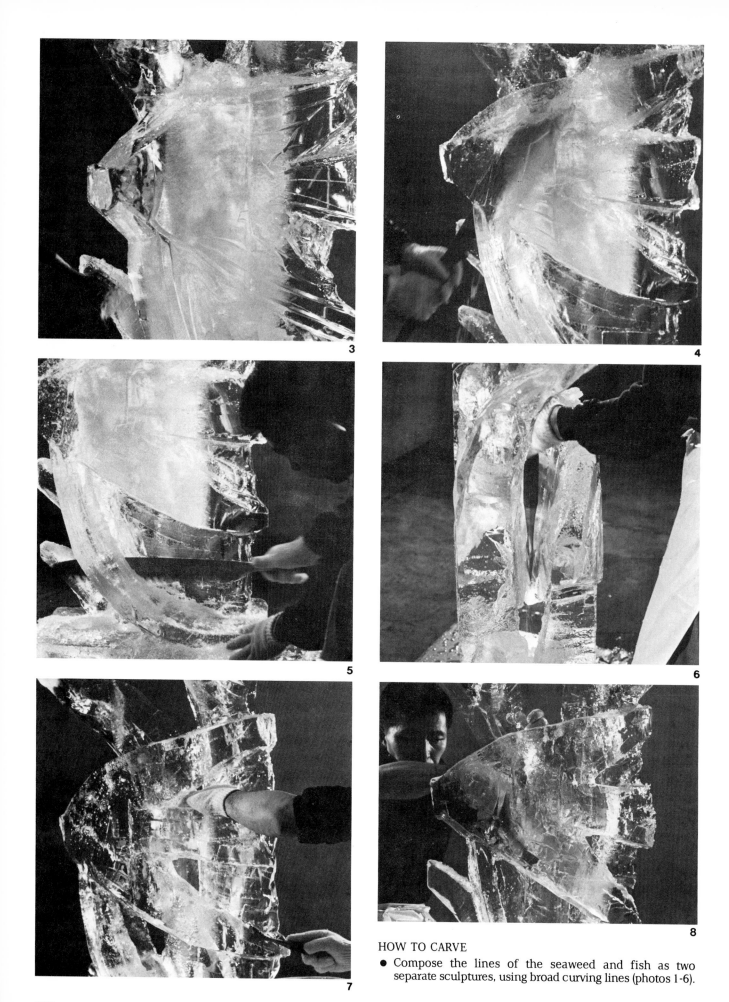

3

4

5

6

7

8

HOW TO CARVE
● Compose the lines of the seaweed and fish as two separate sculptures, using broad curving lines (photos 1-6).

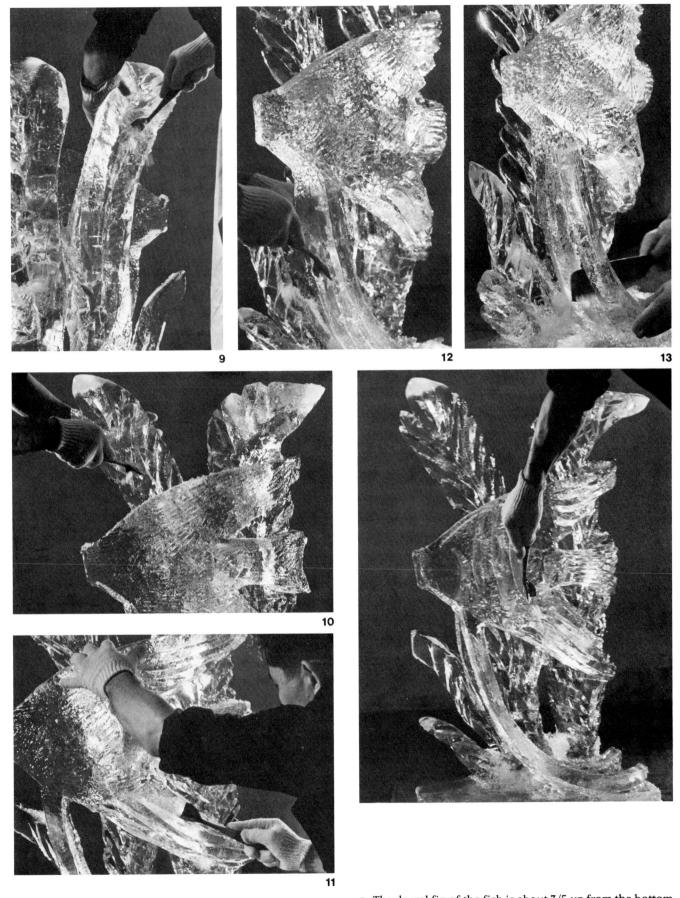

9

12

13

10

11

- The piece will be dull if the lines are too regular, so make them asymetrical and curving (photos 7-14).

- The dorsal fin of the fish is about 3/5 up from the bottom of the seaweed.
- The last parts to be done are the trailing pectoral fins, as they are so fragile.

10 波に鯉

CARP ON A WAVE

Ice 1 Piece

This carp on top of a wave is rather dramatic. It represents the strong carp ascending a swift stream, it's actions frozen for an instant.

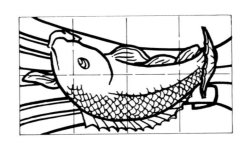

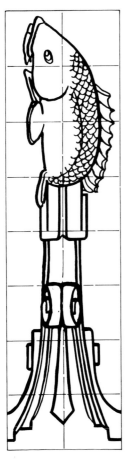

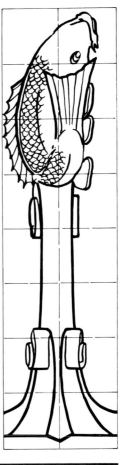

2

3

4

6

7

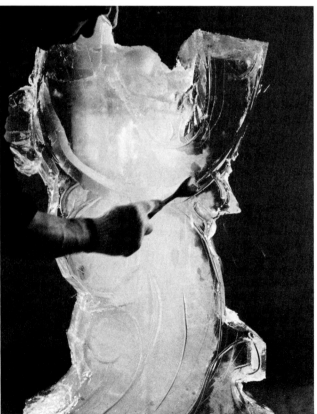

5

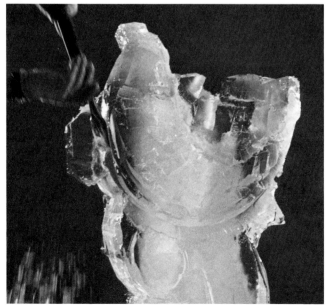

8

HOW TO CARVE

● When making the drawing, divide the ice into eights; 5/8 for the wave and 3/8 for the carp. If this ratio is altered, the piece loses its balance, and the sense of power is lost.

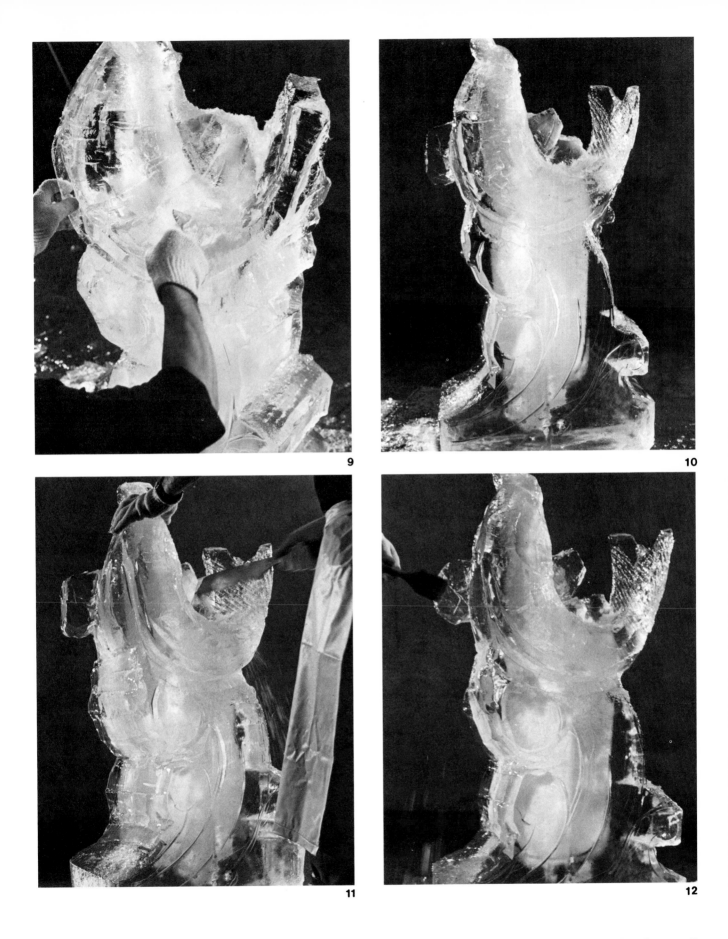

9

10

11

12

- The tail is curved to emphasize the fish's strength.
- It is better to have the whole piece roughed out, than to go into too much detail (photos 1-10).

- The scale of the carp is not that important, but the overall balance of the carp and wave is (photos 12-22).

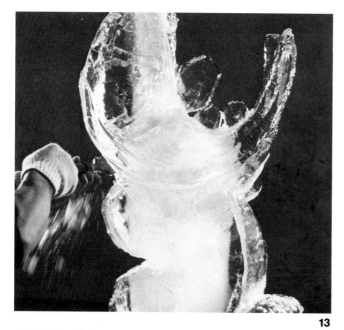

13

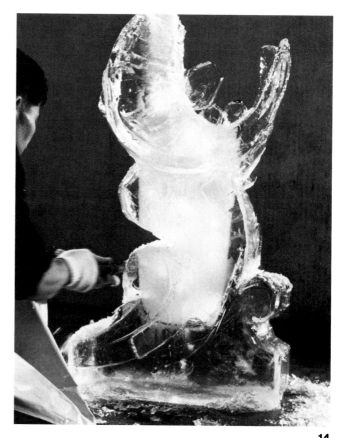

14

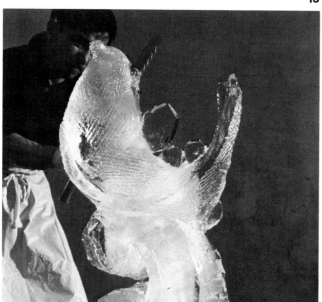

15

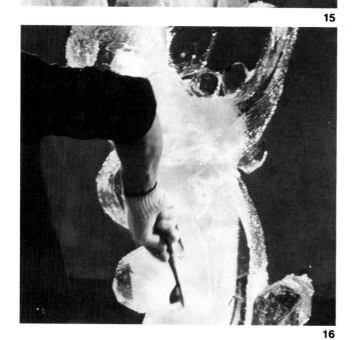

16

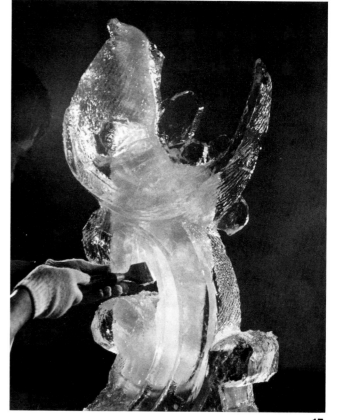

17

18

19

20

22

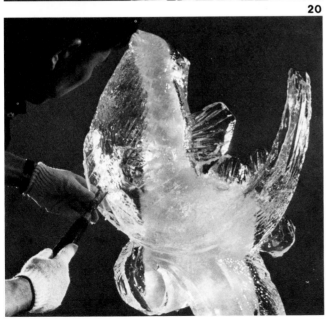

21

11 藻の中を泳ぐ金魚

GOLD FISH

Ice 1 Piece

The goldfish has an egg-shaped body and a unique tail. This swimming fish is flitting about in the water, which is the impression you should try to achieve.

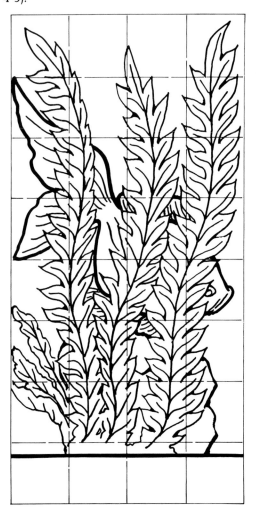

HOW TO CARVE

● The tail and pectoral fins are connected to the seaweed. Do the upper part of the seaweed first, then the seaweed around the fish (photos 1-3), and the fish itself last (photos 4-9).

1

2

3

6

4

7

5

● Bring out the characteristicly wide tail and body carefully (photos 7-10). It is necessary to use the chisel on both the seaweed and the fish with skill and delicacy.

8

9

10

11

- Carefully etch the scales on the carp with the angle chisel.

12 牡牛

BULL

Ice 1/2 A Cut

It is a pleasant sight to see such rural scenes as cattle grazing in wide fields. This bull has his head raised high. You should try to express the bull's strength.

1

2

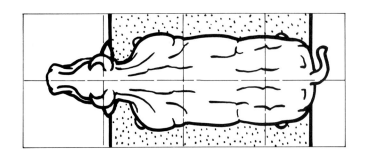

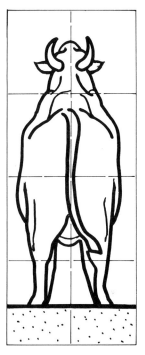

HOW TO CARVE

● The legs are done last, after the torso and head. The legs are thin when finished, so beware of breaking them.

3

4

5

8

6

9

7

10

● Carve the head, torso, and legs in the proportions shown
  (photos 1-6).

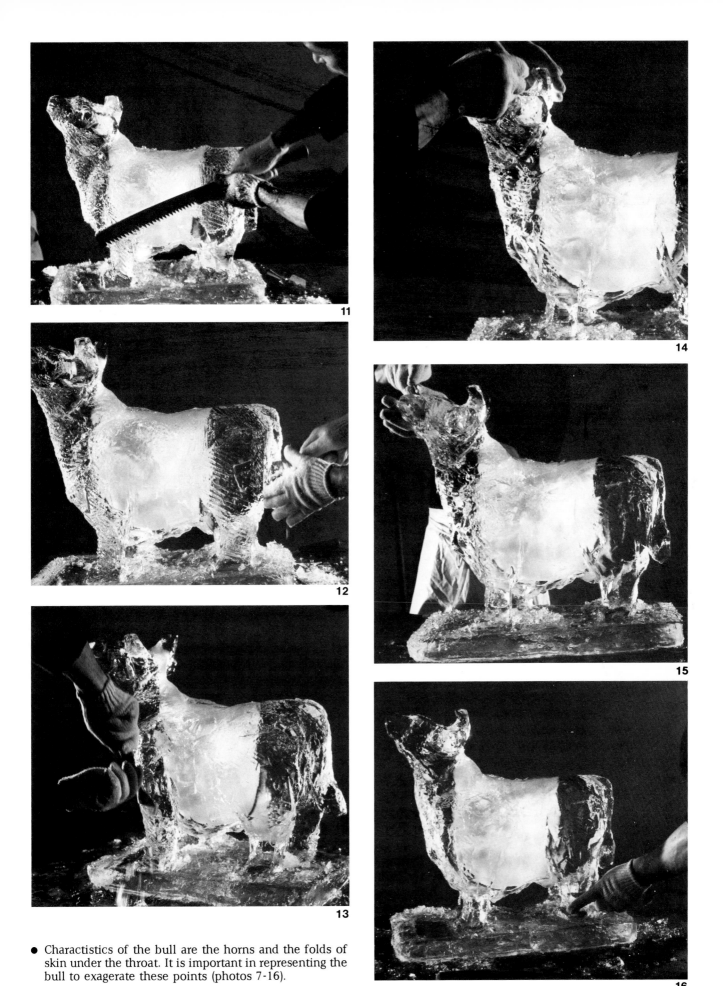

● Charactistics of the bull are the horns and the folds of skin under the throat. It is important in representing the bull to exagerate these points (photos 7-16).

13 きつね

FOX

Ice ¾ Cut

The fox is a member of the dog family. Its general shape is about the same as a dog's except for the longer, more sharply pointed nose. By having the fox crouch down, with the face extended, you express the idea of the fox being a wild creature of the woods.

1

2

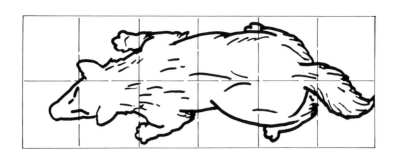

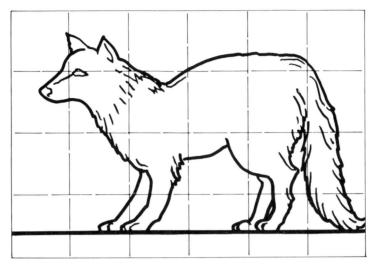

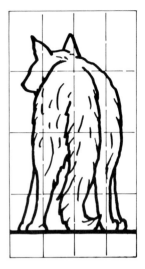

HOW TO CARVE

● The main characteristics of the fox are a slender nose and a tail which is thicker towards the tip.

● These points are exagerated, following the steps in photos 1-5.

3

4

5

6

7

8

- When carving the front legs, do not take off too much ice (photos 5 and 6).

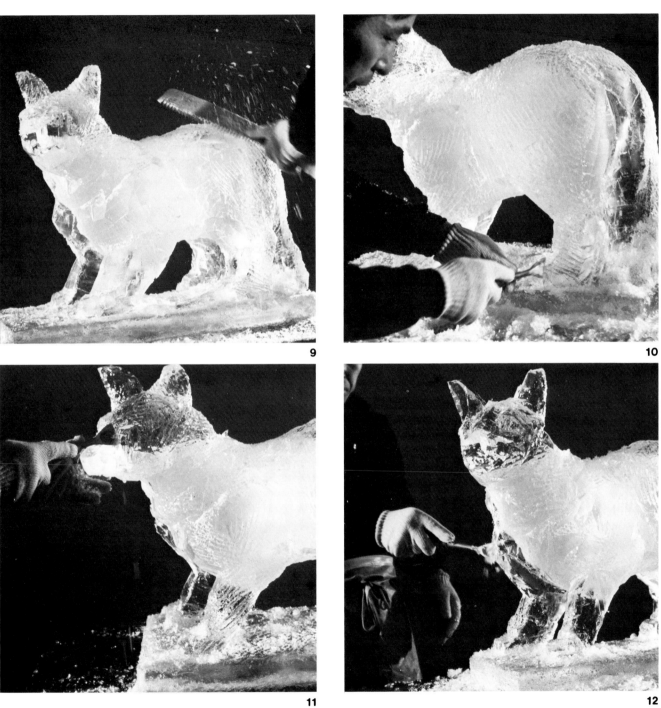

9

10

11

12

● The face of the fox should be long and pointed, and the tail wide and bushy (photo 8-11).

● When finishing the body, from the neck to the chest, refer to photo 12.

14 鹿―I

DEER ― I

Ice 1 Piece

There are many kinds of deer living in Honshu, Kokkaido and Shikoku, each of which have different characteristics such as antler shape and fur coloring. Some do not have antlers at all. This deer is close to the caribou or reindeer. I have made this one with high, wide antlers; big, soft eyes; and long, slim legs. These are emphasized, of course.

1

2

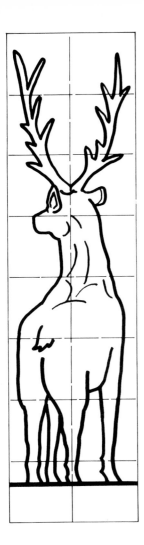
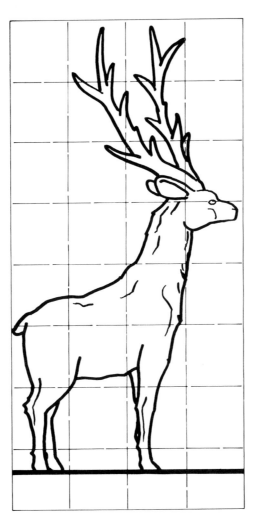
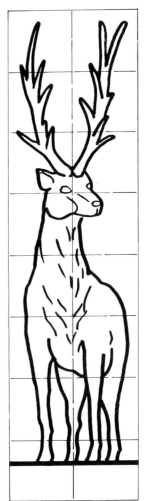

HOW TO CARVE

- The legs are carved just like those of the other animals, but, of course, are more slender.

3

4

5

8

6

9

7

- The antlers are emphasized, and should be sharply pointed (photos 1-6).
- As the end point of the deer, the tail greatly influences the final result.

10

11

12

13

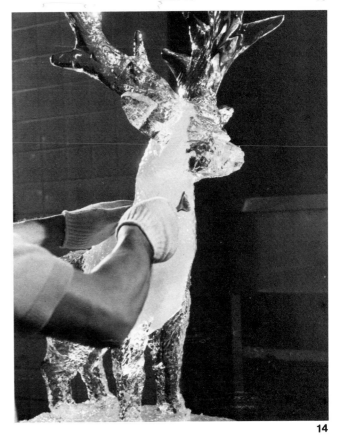

14

● Gradually carve out the legs, head, and torso, being careful not to work too fast (photos 7-14).

15 鹿—II

DEER — II

Ice 1 Piece

This deer is very similar to "Deer — I," but as it is lying down, it is easier to balance. The body is not high, and the neck and back are slightly arched. If the line from throat to the lower chest is not done well, the finished result will be poor.

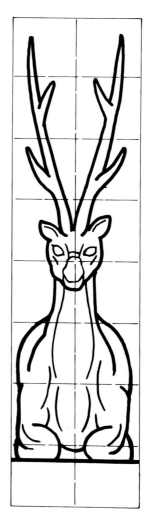 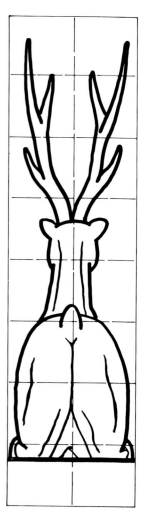

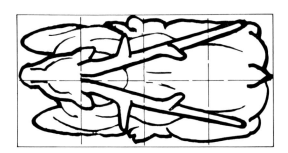

1

2

3

4

5

6

7

HOW TO CARVE

● The antlers are carved as in "Deer − I" (photos 1-5). Be careful in making the curves of the antlers.

8

9

10

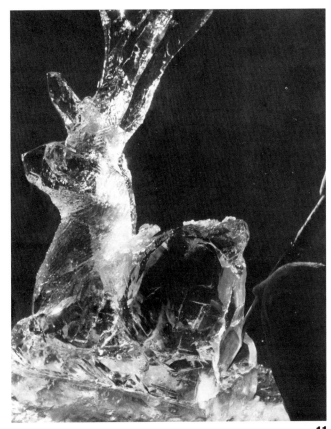

11

12

● Next, do the face and chest. The stand is done last (photos 6-12). Be careful when rounding the back and tail.

16 馬

HORSE

Ice 7/8 Cut

The horse is a difficult theme. The back haunches and withers are particularly hard, and, for the size of its body, it has very slender legs. The problem is how to do this properly and assure good results.

1

2

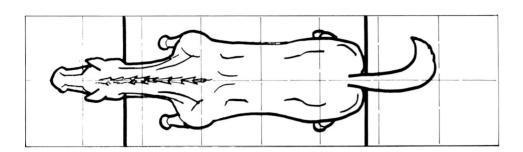

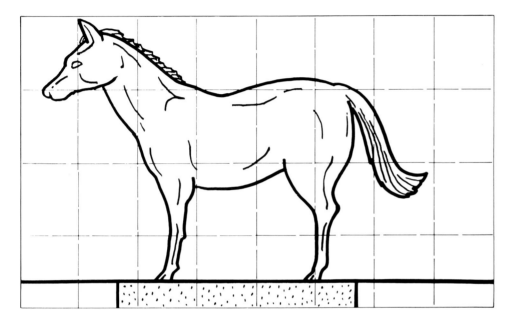

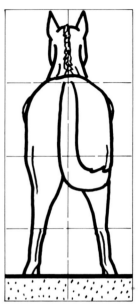

HOW TO CARVE

● After roughing out the body, make a smooth line from the base of the neck to the haunches (photos 1-10).

3

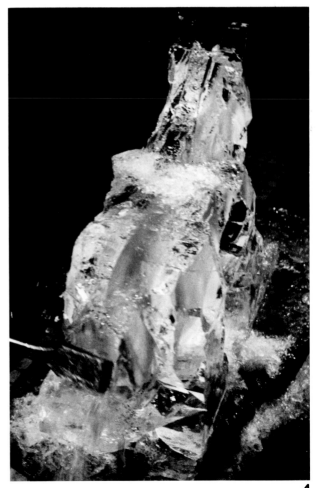

4

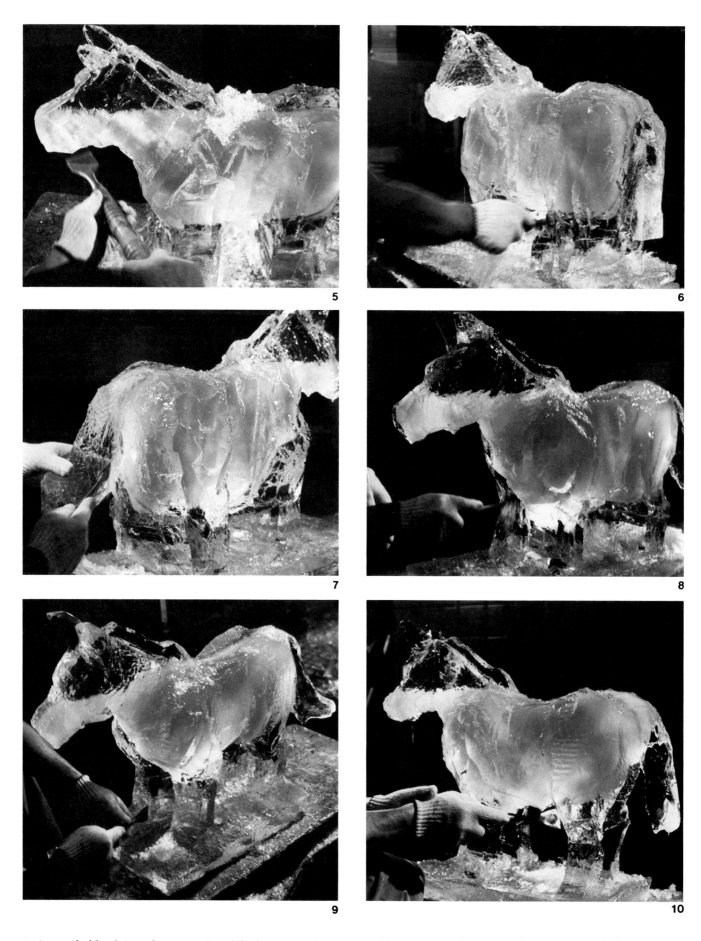

5

6

7

8

9

10

● A rounded back is a characteristic of the horse. The legs should be long and slender.

● The ears are pointed, and the mane extends from head to shoulders (photos 11 and 12).

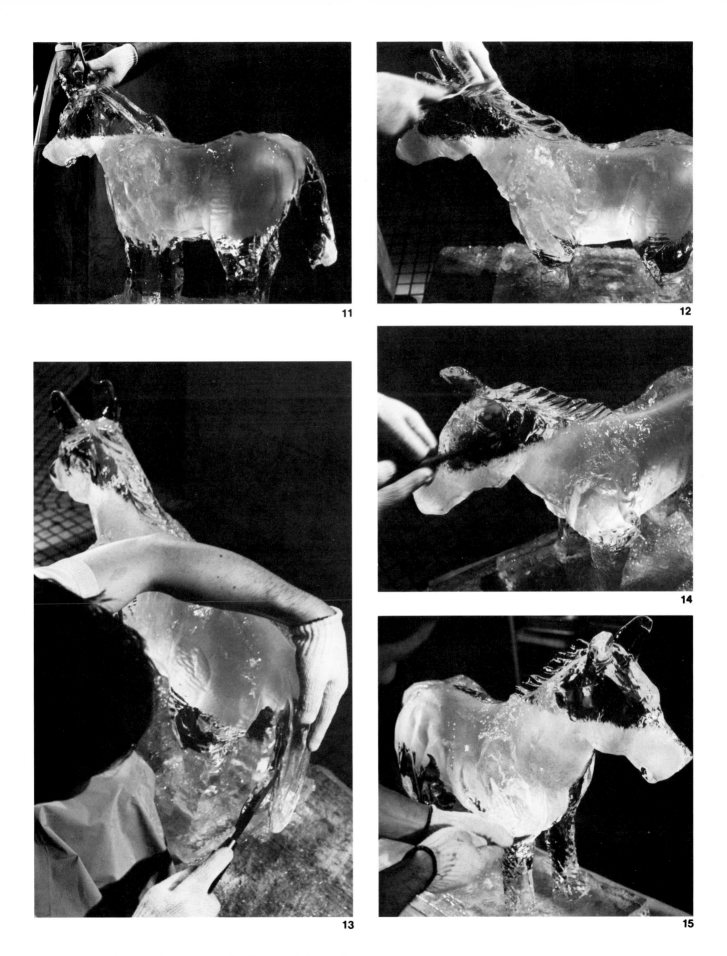

11

12

13

14

15

● The finished tail is a key point, and is done with the angle chisel (photo 13).

17 犬
DOG

Ice 1/2 A Cut

There are many kinds of dogs. Compared to the fox and deer, the dog has short legs and a relatively short neck. The dog's nose is not as sharp as that of the fox.

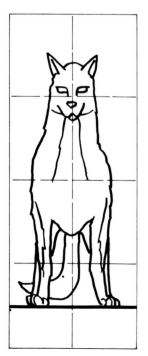
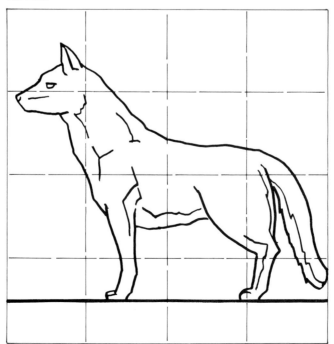
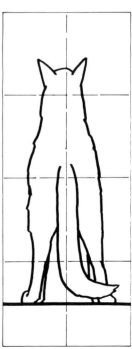

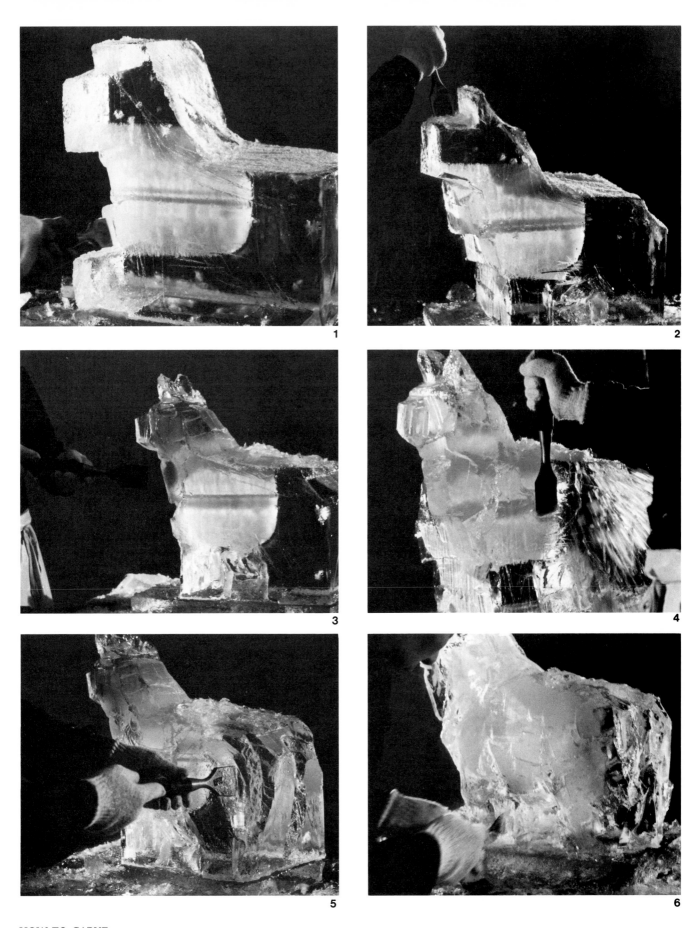

HOW TO CARVE
● After deciding on the shape of the head, the whole figure
  should be balanced (photos 1-5).

7

8

9

10

11

12

● The legs should be done carefully. First, form the line from the front of the chest to the forelegs, then form the shoulder line from the back through the tail to the back legs. Next, do the back, and then finish the lower chest down between the legs (photos 6-10).

18 ハープ

HARP

Ice ½ B Cut

The harp is an Occidental musical instrument that has been used for centuries. I think that this representation is quite elegant.

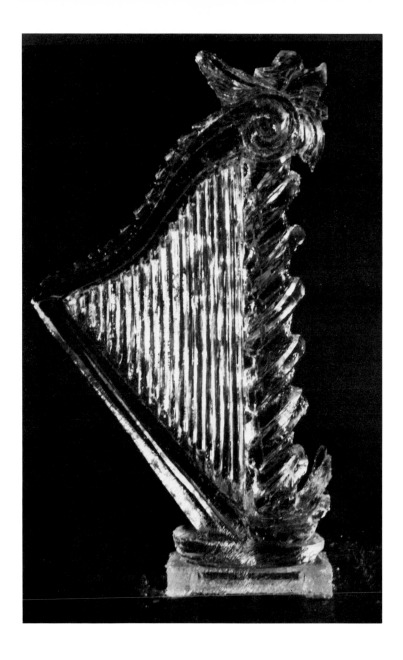

1

2

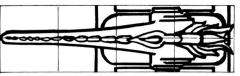

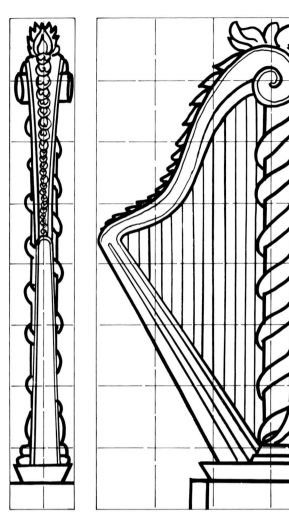

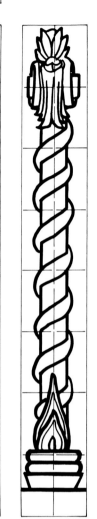

3

4

5

6

7

8

HOW TO CARVE
- The harp should be stable and balanced properly on the stand. If the stand is too large, the result will be poor.
- Lay the ice on its side, and cut out the outline (photos 1-8).

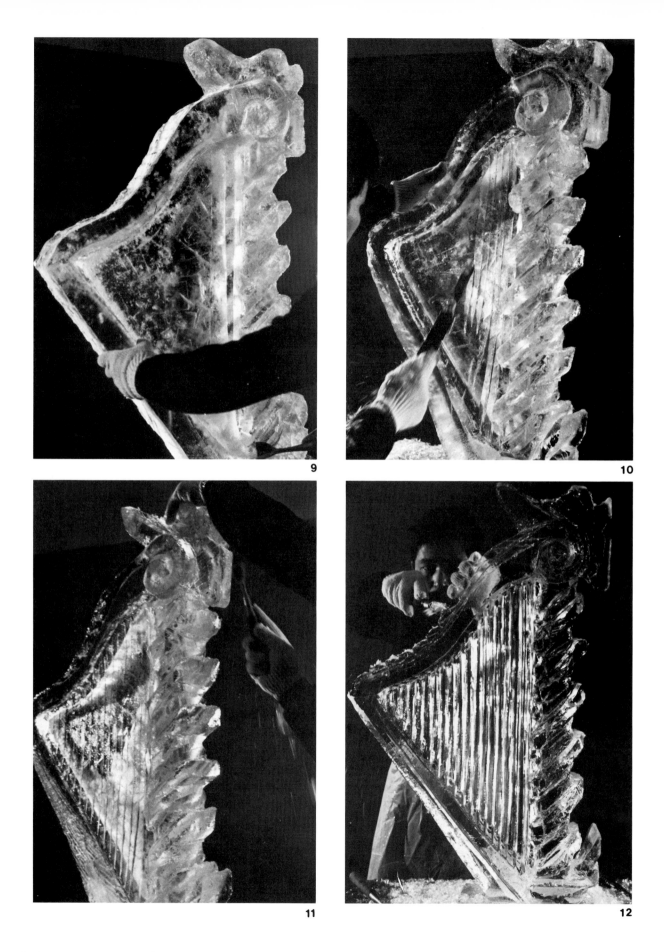

9

10

11

12

- The harp strings are all the same width and depth. To do this, the area between the frames must be flat and smooth (photos 9-10).
- Finish the border decoration last (photos 11-12).

19 寿

KOTOBUKI
(Long Life/Congratulations)

Ice ½ B Cut

This is frequently used in Japan for congratulatory dinner parties. At these times, this Japanese character is especially appropriate.

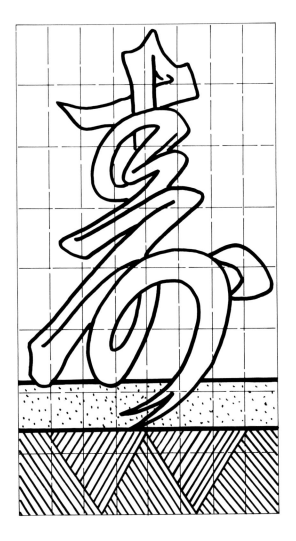

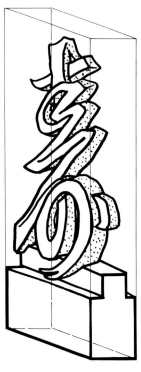

1

2

3

4

5

6

HOW TO CARVE
- This character should be carved in the same manner as it is written with a brush. The width of the individual lines should be steady and even.

7

9

8

10

- The character should be steady on its stand.
- The character is first shaped roughly, worked with the ice on its side, and then finished when upright (photos 1-10).

20 MERRY X'MAS

Ice 2½ B Cut

This carving, along with the traditional Christmas decorations such as Christmas trees and flowers, evokes the spirit of Christmas at Christmas parties.

1

2

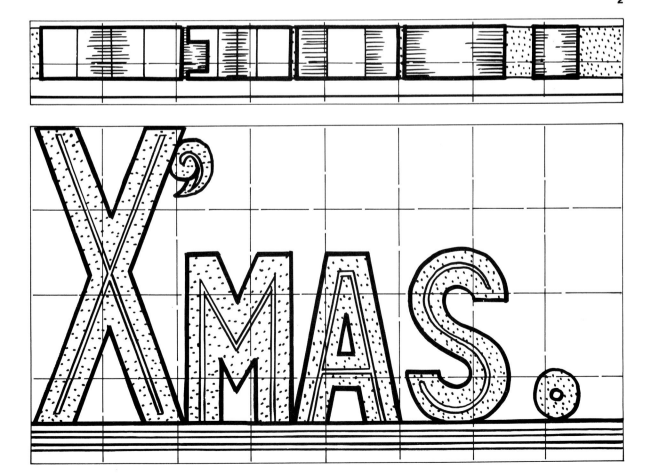

HOW TO CARVE
● As this is made from two blocks of ice, carefully check the dimensions of each. Then proceed by etching the letters on the ice (photos 1-4).
● The side of each letter should be carved in clean, straight lines (photos 5-14).

9

10

11

12

13

14

● Be sure that the large letters are of equal heights and that the small letters are of equal heights.

21 貝殻を持つ少年

BOY HOLDING A SHELL

Ice 1 Piece

This has a young boy holding a shell over his head. One main point to remember is the balance of the shell to the boy's body. You can put flowers or fruit in the shell, as there is ample room for them.

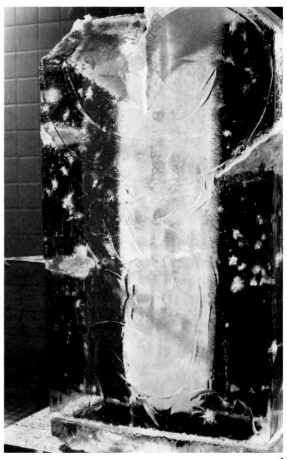

1

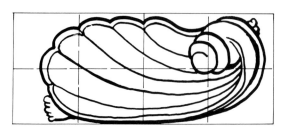

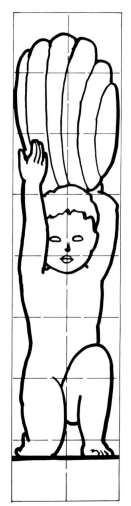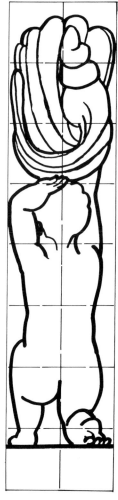

2

3

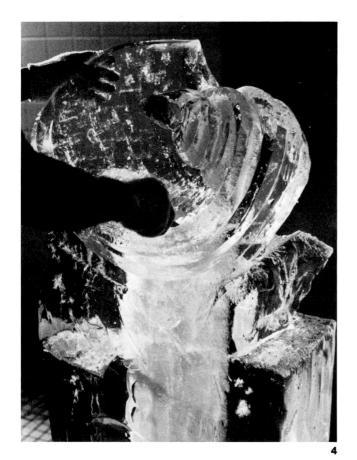

4

6

5

7

HOW TO CARVE
- Follow the proportions as shown in the drawing, for if they are not maintained, the figure will be out of balance. For example, if the shell is made too big, the boy's figure will seem over-burdened, and if it is made too small, the boy will appear too large. Therefore, be careful when

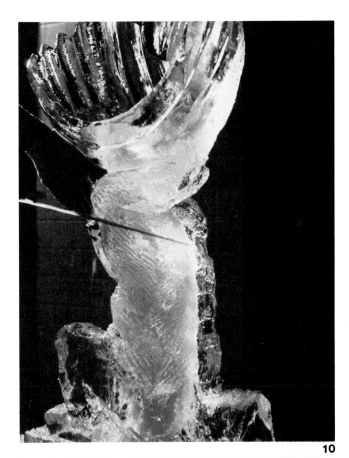

8

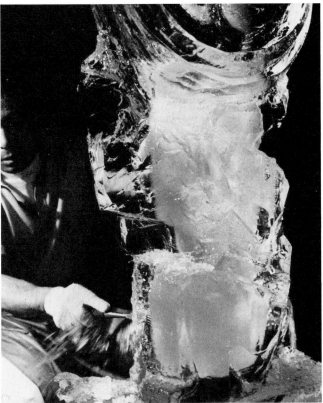

9

10

working out the proportions (photos 1-3).

● Rough out the shape of the shell, then the boy (photos 4-11).

● The important lines on the boy are from neck to back and from neck to stomach; if these curves are altered, the boy will have a flat, expressionless figure.

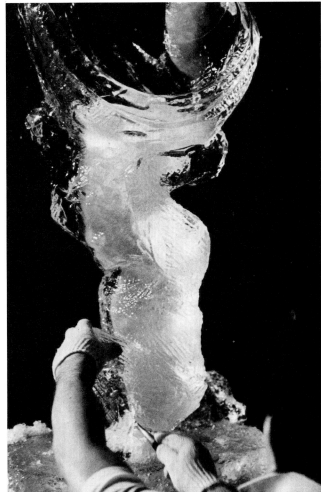

11

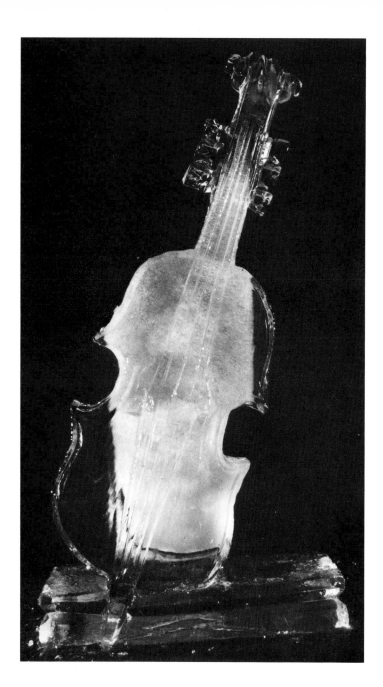

22 チェロ

CELLO

Ice 1 Piece

The shape of this cello is simple, but it has the beauty of symetry.

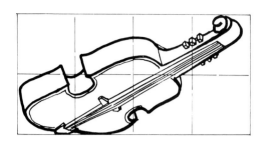

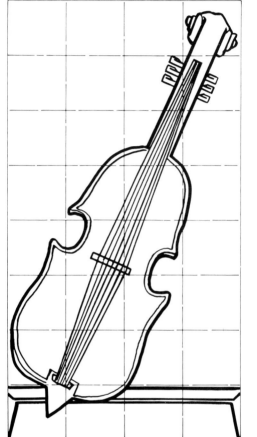

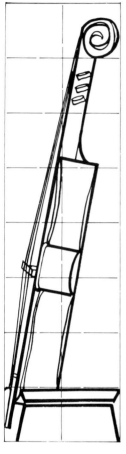

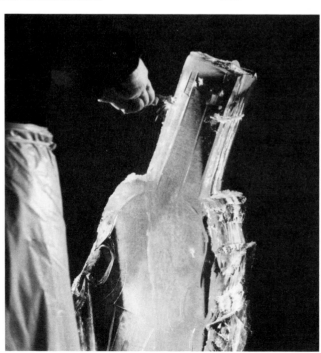

2

3

4

6

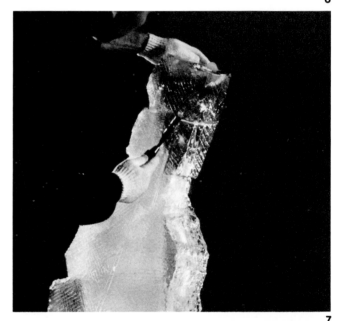

7

5

8

HOW TO CARVE
- The cello is perfectly symmetrical on each side, with the strings being the center line. Because of this, each side

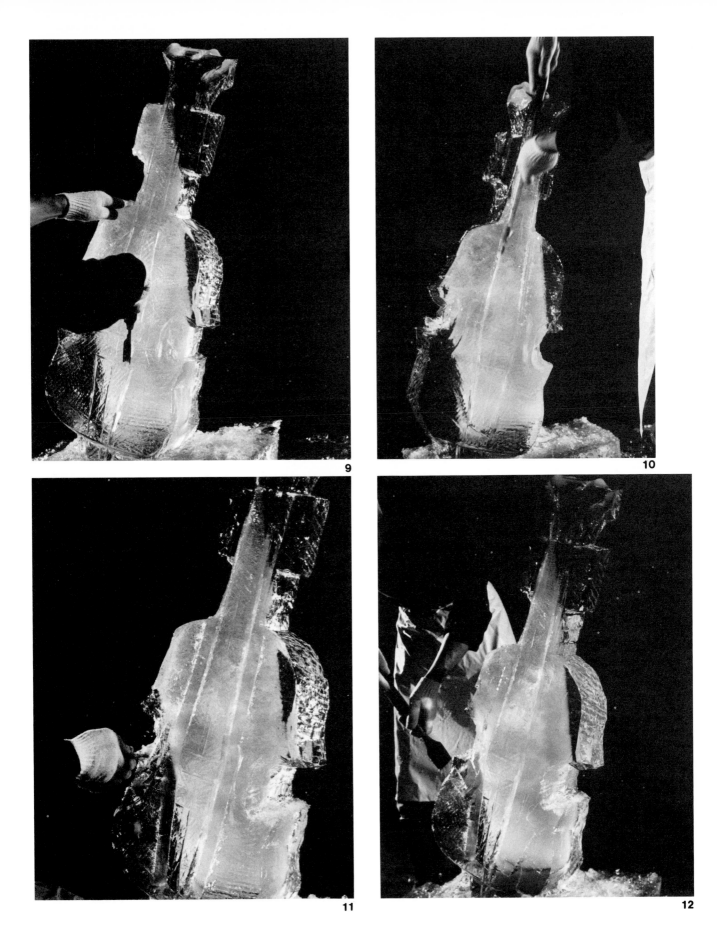

9

10

11

12

must be carved the same, or the symmetry will be destroyed. The strings must be done skillfully (photos 1-16).

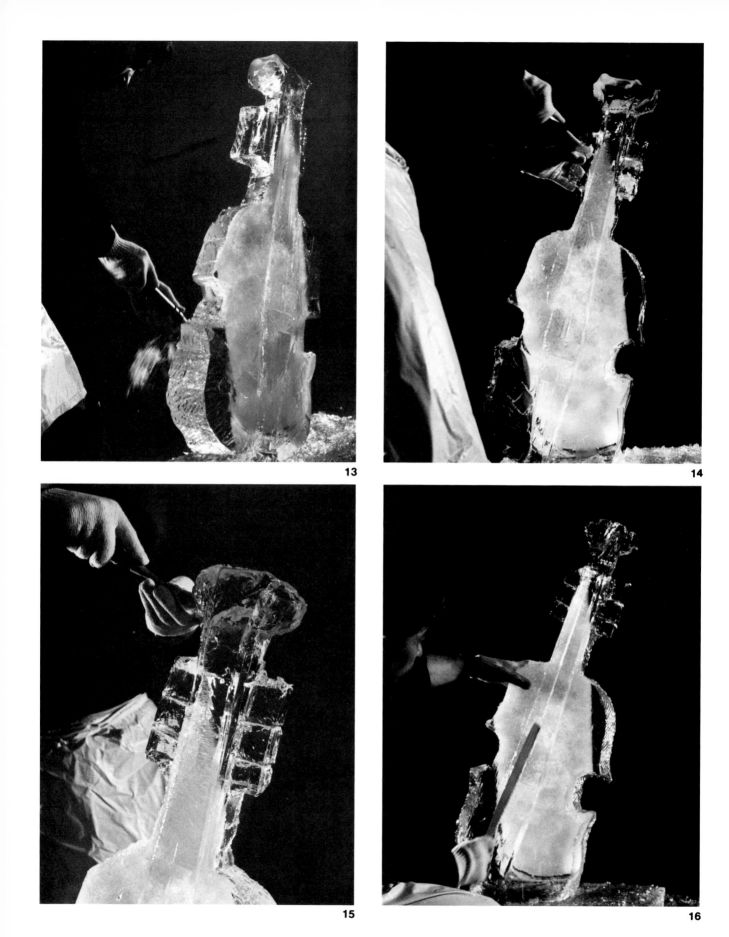

13

14

15

16

● The profile of the instrument should be a gentle curve. Be careful not to make it too flat (photos 11-16).

23 小便小僧

SMALL BOY

Ice ½ A Cut

I wanted to make a cute little boy and to do this, I made the boy's head and stomach large, and the legs short and thick.

1

2

245

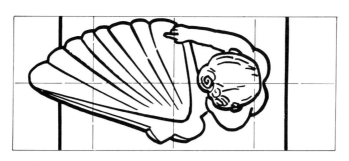

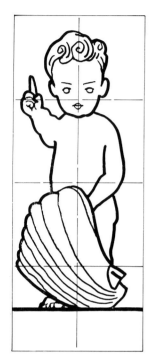
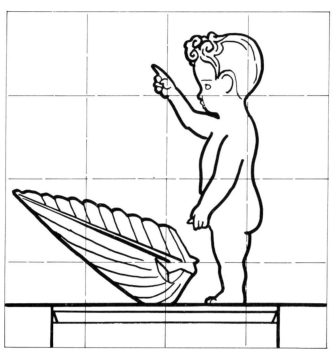
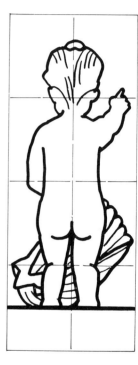

3

4

5

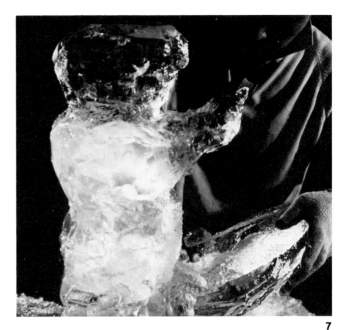

7

8

6

9

HOW TO CARVE
● The human figure is quite difficult. In the case of children, the figure will be more child-like if the previously stated points are emphasized. The lines and curves should be soft and rounded, without angular surfaces (photos 1-13).

10

11

12

13

- The arms are short. Be sure that both are the same length.
- The important areas are the face, head, back, and waist, which should be rounded (photos 8-13).

24 鯉と器
CARP AND DISH

Ice ¼ A Cut, 2 Pieces

By having a dish under the carp, various cold foods or flowers can be displayed. The bowl under the jumping carp should be large and is decorated with a wave.

1

2

3

4

5

6

7

HOW TO CARVE

● Refer to the "Carp on a Wave," Exercise 10, to do the carp and dish. Do not forget that a basic theme of this piece is the expression of the carp's strength. The tail is pointed up, and the body is arched.

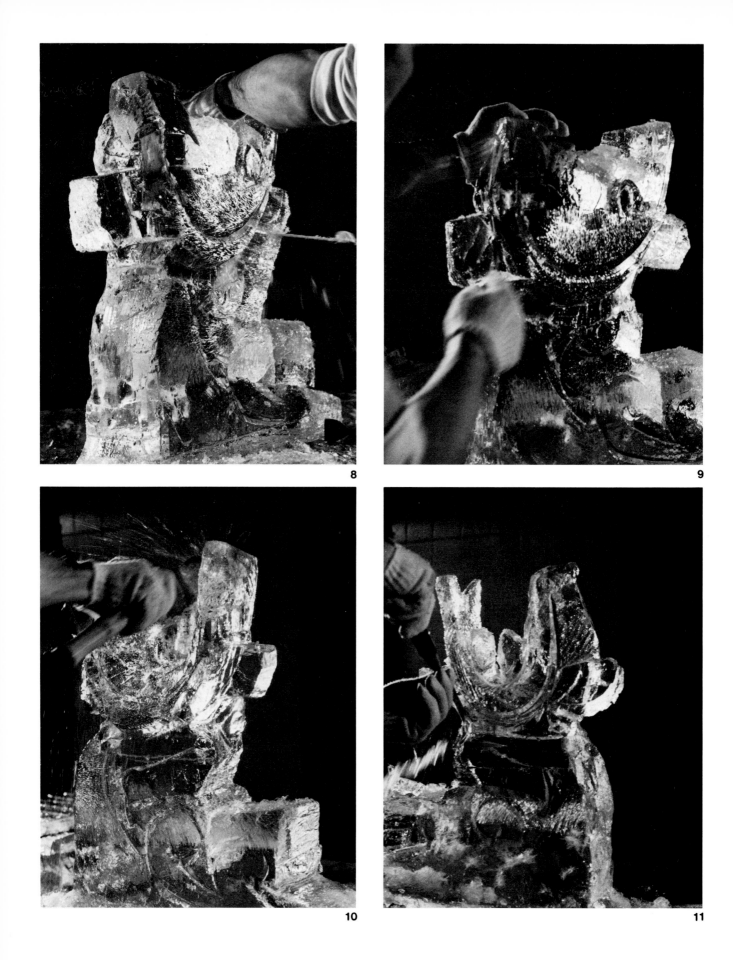

8

9

10

11

● The bowl is made from a flat block of ice with the angle chisel, and the flutings on it are of the same depth and width (photos 1-3). If the flutings are not regular, the overall effect will be poor.

12

13

14

15

25 エンゼル
フィッシュと器

ANGEL FISH AND BOWL

Ice 2, ¼ A Cut

In the center of this round bowl, there is a ball upon which an angel fish is swimming. It is important to balance the bowl, the ball, and the angel fish.

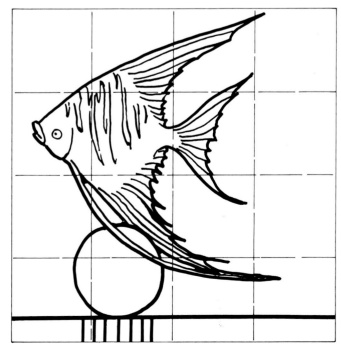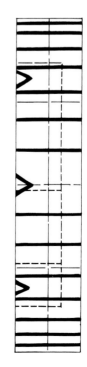

254

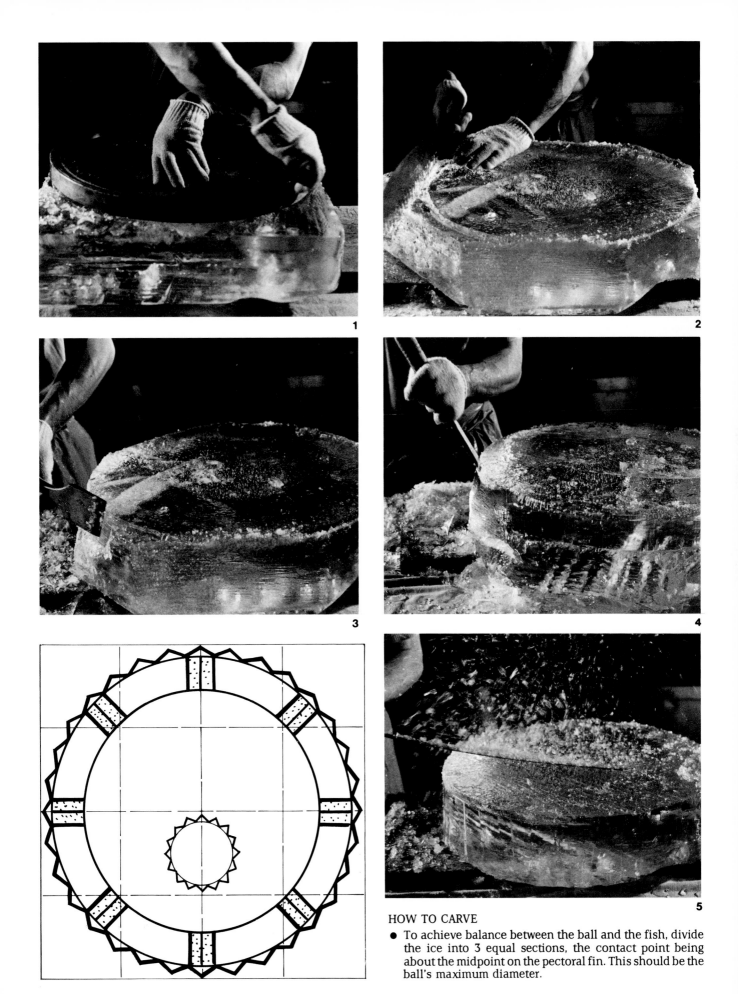

1

2

3

4

5

HOW TO CARVE

- To achieve balance between the ball and the fish, divide the ice into 3 equal sections, the contact point being about the midpoint on the pectoral fin. This should be the ball's maximum diameter.

6

7

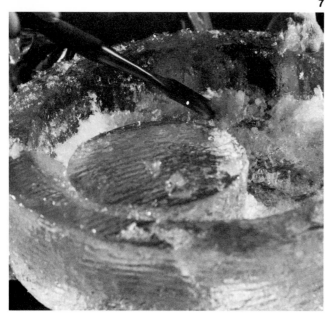

8

9

10

• To make the bowl, etch concentric circles in the proportions shown. Use a compass in making these circles (photos 1-6). Then dig out the center of the bowl, making sure the depth is uniform (photos 7-11).

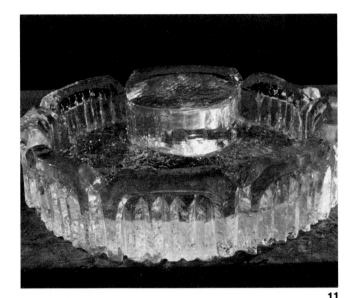

11

13

12

- Refer to "Angel Fish," Exercise 9. Emphasize the tail and fins in detail (photos 12-22).
- When finished, put the angel fish in the bowl.

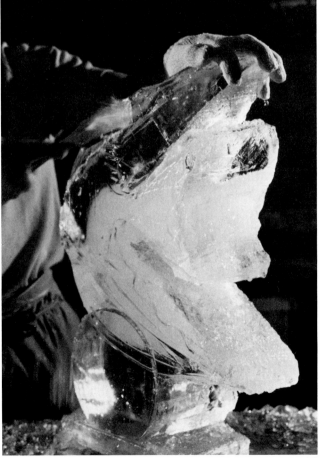

14

15

16

17

18

19

20

21

22

26 スワンと器

SWAN AND BOWL

Ice ½ A Cut, ¼ A Cut

This fan-shaped bowl goes well with the figure of a swan with outstretched wings.

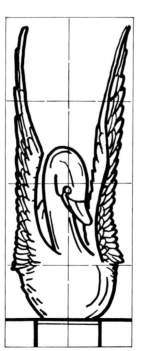

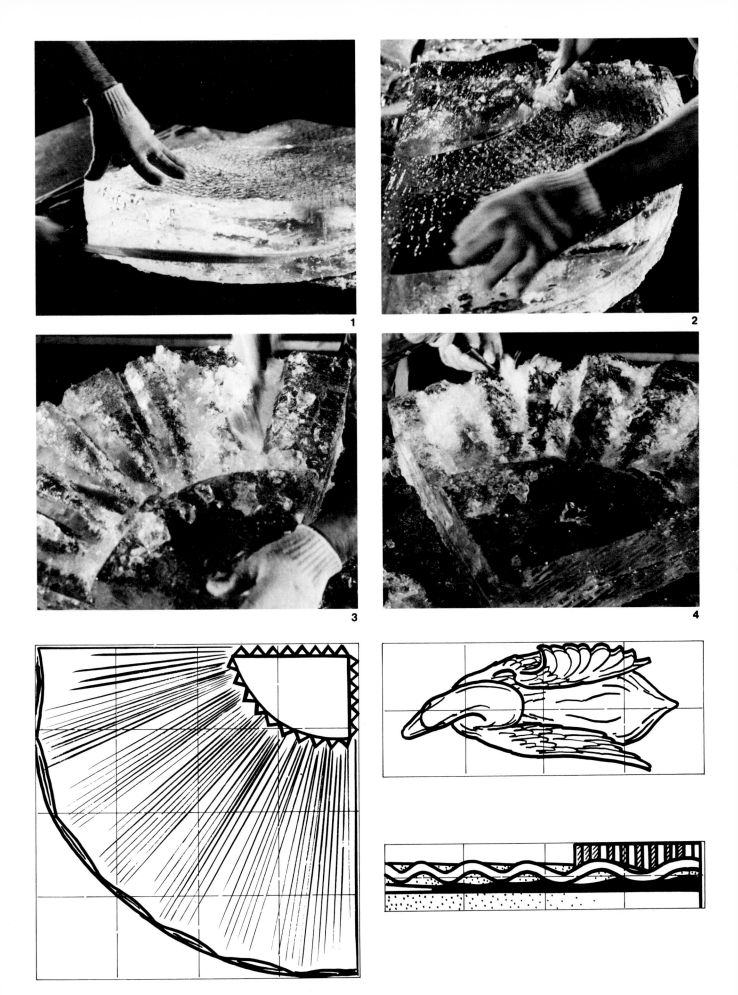

5

8

6

9

7

HOW TO CARVE

● When carving out the fan, make the stand at an angle. The wave pattern on the fan goes from the stand out to the edge, each line forming part of the radius. Use the angle chisel to form the lines, and the flat chisel to dig to the proper depth (photos 1-8).

10

11

12

13

● Refer to "Swan – I" and "Swan – II," Exercises 3 and 4. Be careful in carving the angle of the beak, wings, and neck (photos 9-12).

❻ 組合せ作品

COMBINED PIECES

1 ジェット旅客機

JET AIRPLANE

Ice 2 Pieces

In this age of space ships and jet airplanes, this airplane, when placed on the main table of a dinner party, will cause people to dream of flying to far away places. It will particularly please younger children. You should use sharp, thin tools when making this airplane.

Fuselage, side view

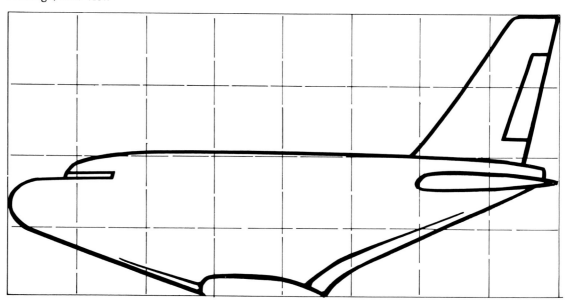

Wings, top view

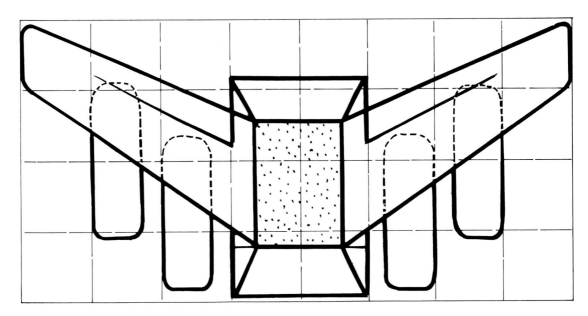

Wings, front view

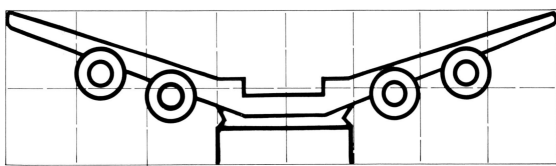

Fuselage, front view

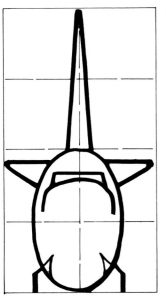

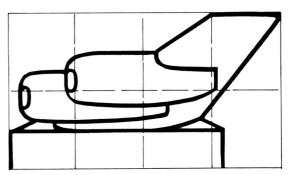

Wings, side view

Fuselage, top view

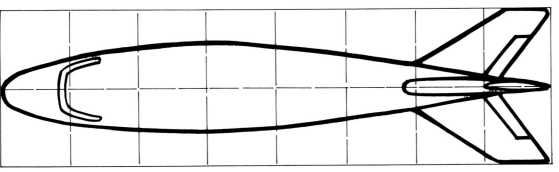

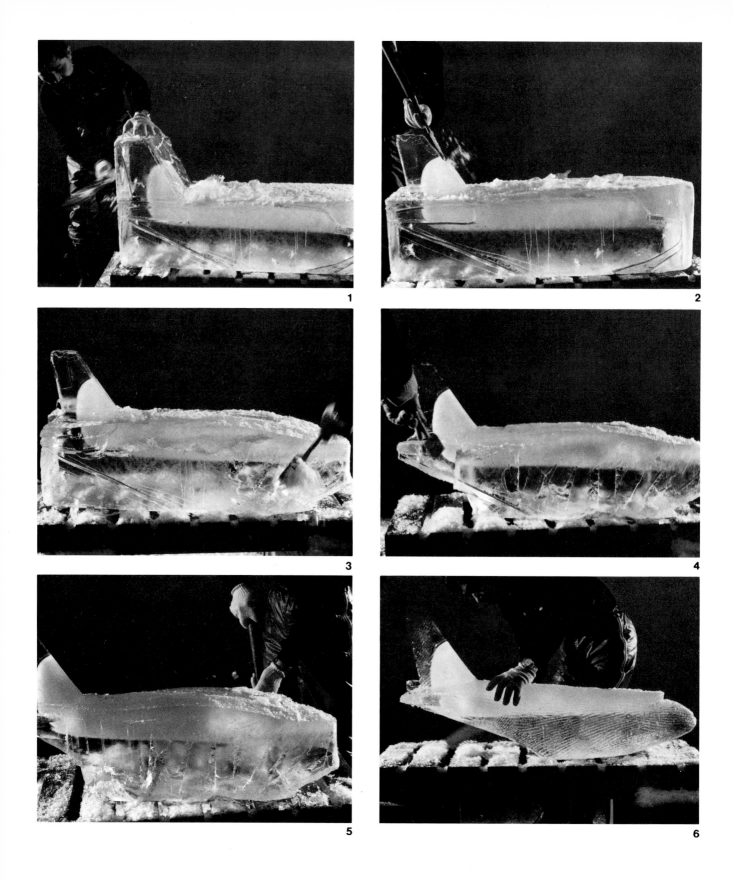

1

2

3

4

5

6

HOW TO CARVE

● As the wings and fuselage are in two separate pieces, this piece is difficult to balance. Make the preliminary etchings as exact as possible to make the wing length and thickness proportional to the fuselage thickness.

Fuselage

(1) Cut away all unnecessary ice with the saw (photo 1).
(2) Rough out the shape of the fuselage with the flat chisel (photos 2 and 3).
(3) Cut out the tail with the flat chisel (photo 4).
(4) Work the fuselage to the correct thickness by carefully

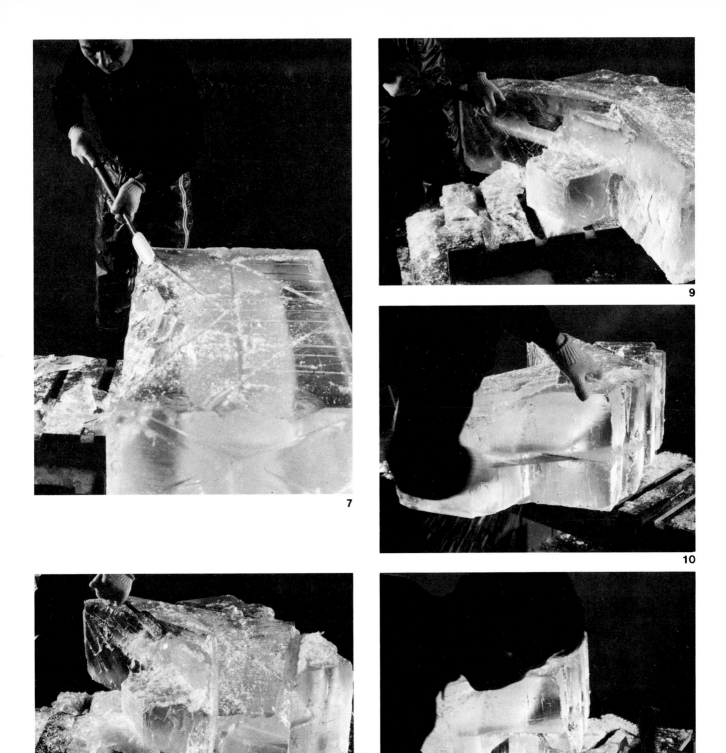

7

9

10

8

11

using the flat chisel (photo 5).
(5) Using the saw, very lightly etch the entire fuselage to give a solid appearance (photo 6).
Wings
(6) Etch the outlines of the wings, engines, and stand on the other block of ice.
(7) Using the flat chisel, rough out the wings (photo 7). Be careful of details such as the engines and stand; use the flat chisel carefully. The engines and stand should be cut out with the saw, then trimmed with the chisel.

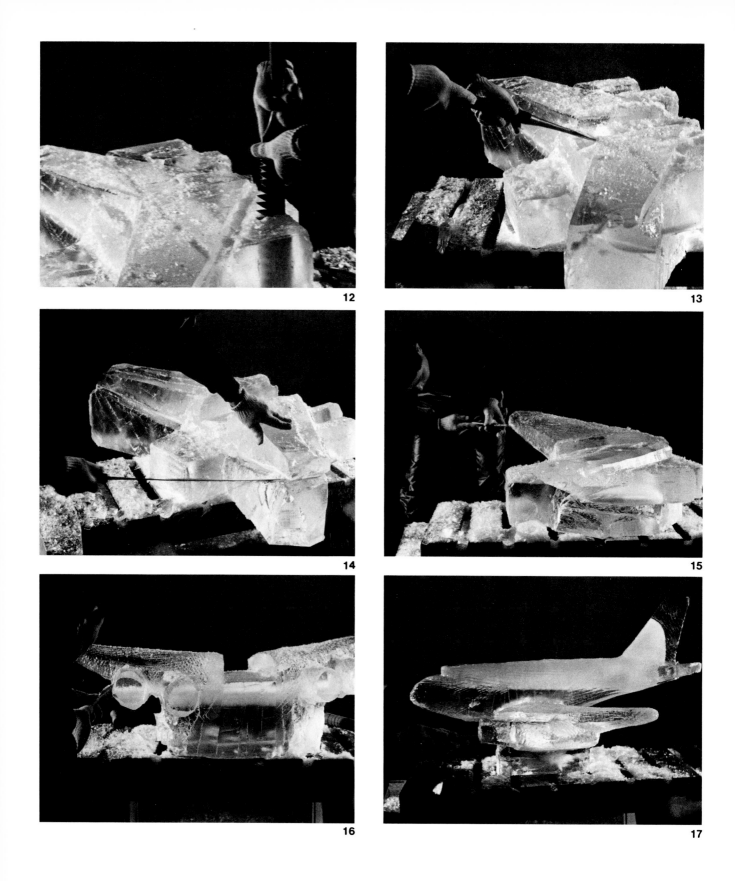

12

13

14

15

16

17

(8) Make the gap to hold the fuselage (photo 13).
(9) Cut off the excess wing thickness with the saw (photo 14).
(10) Check the overall balance and shape, then finish the details with the chisel (photos 15 and 16). Then, with the saw, etch the surface of the wing like the fuselage.

Assembly
(11) Place the fuselage in the space provided for it on the top of the wings (photo 17).

② クラシックカー

CAR

Ice 1 Piece, 2 B Cuts

This is a car of classic style. Compared to the present automobiles, which are functional, characterless, and mobile deadly weapons, this classic car has a quaint charm.

Car body

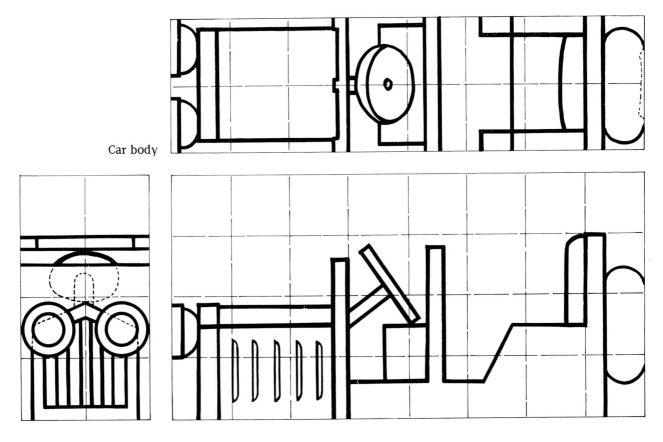

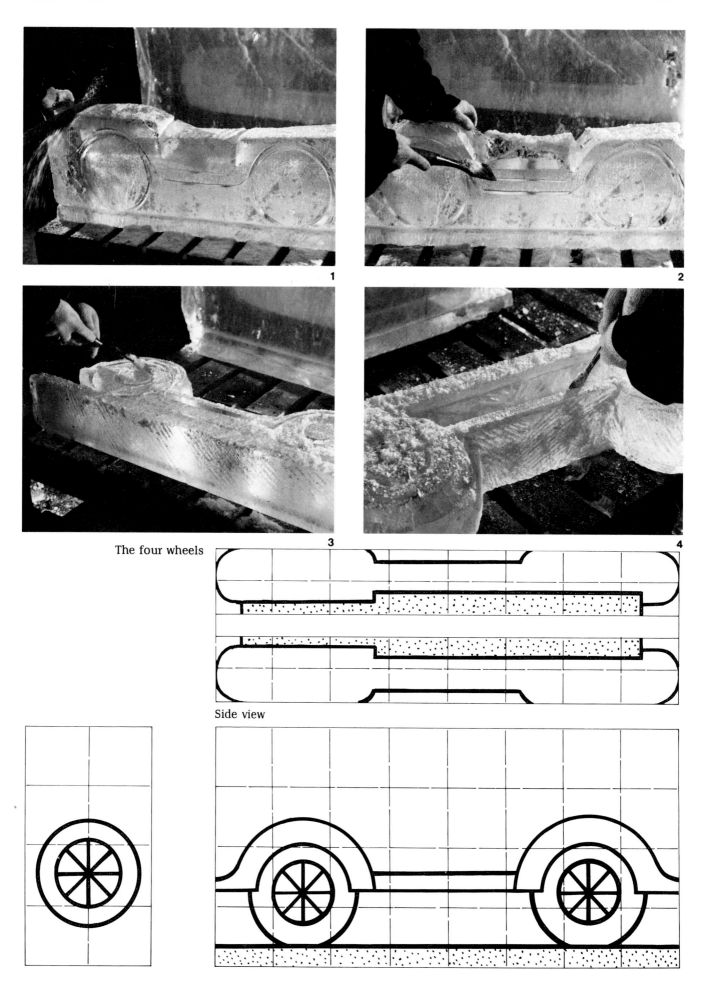

1

2

3

4

The four wheels

Side view

5

6

7

8

OBJECTIVES
- The wheels are all the same size. The area between the wheels is used for the chassis.
- The excess ice is cut away with the saw, and should not be too difficult.

HOW TO CARVE
(1) On each B cut, etch the front and back wheels, the fenders, and the running board, then cut away excess ice (photo 1).
(2) With the flat chisel, cut out the outline (photo 2).
(3) The line between the fender and the tire should be clear (photo 3).
(4) Carve out the space between the running board and the stand (photo 4).

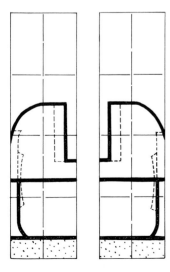

Front and rear view of wheels

9

273

10

11

12

13

14

(5) Round out the fenders, then finish the tires and running boards.
(6) Both sides are made in the same way. When compared to each other, they are identical (photos 5-7).
(7) Cut away excess ice from the body with the saw (photo 8).
(8) Using the flat chisel, make the head lamps (photo 9).

(9) Make the back seat and spare tire in the back of the car (photos 10-12).
(10) Make the windshield, front seat, and the final work on the headlamps, then etch deep lines on the hood, as shown (photos 13 and 14).
(11) The body then is placed over the wheels.

③ 龍

DRAGON   Ice 4 Pieces; 5½ B Cuts; ¼ A Cut; 1/6 B Cut

The dragon is an imaginary animal of ancient China, and can be considered to be somewhat like a reptile. It is usually composed of various different animals. The body is like that of a snake, the horns are like those of a deer, the eyes are like those of a devil, and the ears are like those of a cow, and it has four legs.

HOW TO CARVE

- The etching must be accurate, or the figure will easily come off balance. Be very careful in this step.
- After the complete carving is assembled, then final touch ups can be made.
- The dragon's head is the most important segment. It should be left a bit rough.

1

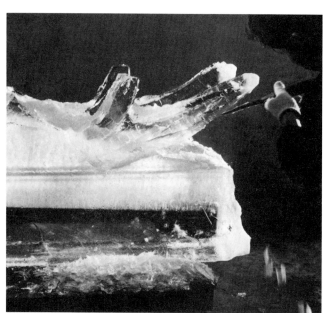

2

3

4

5

6

7

The Dragon's Head   Ice 1 Piece

(1) First, cut the outline with the saw, then make the horns (photo 1).
(2) Round off the head (photo 2).
(3) Slowly shape the back of the head with the saw (photo 3).
(4) Carve the profile and the eyes (photo 4).
(5) Do the nose, then make the barbels (photo 5).
(6) Carve the ears, eyes, head and upper lips (photo 6).
(7) Carve out the mouth with the saw (photo 7).
(8) Carve the lower jaw (photo 8).

8

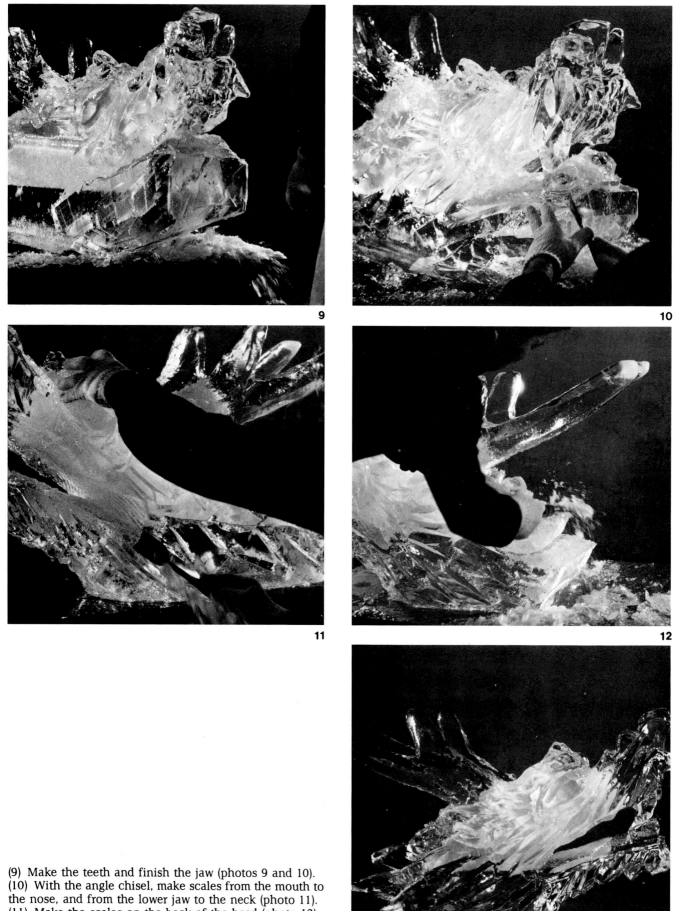

9

10

11

12

13

(9) Make the teeth and finish the jaw (photos 9 and 10).
(10) With the angle chisel, make scales from the mouth to the nose, and from the lower jaw to the neck (photo 11).
(11) Make the scales on the back of the head (photo 12).
(12) Finish the head with the flat chisel, using sharp, angular lines (photo 13).

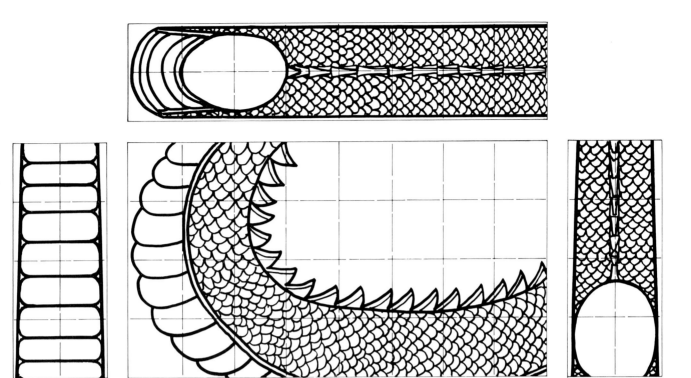

The Dragon's Body   Ice 2 Pieces

(1) Make sure the mating surfaces of the two blocks of ice
are smooth, etch the profile, then cut away excess ice with
the saw (photo 14).
(2) Round off the lower part and shape the back, leaving the
back fin (photo 15).

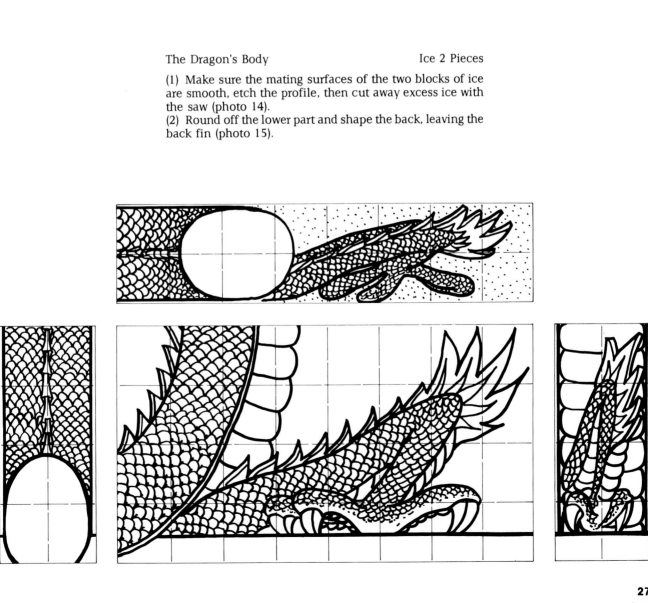

14

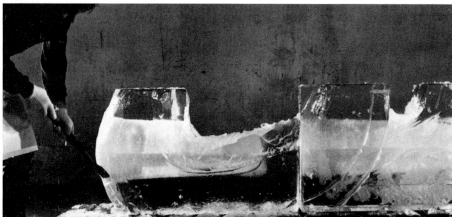

15

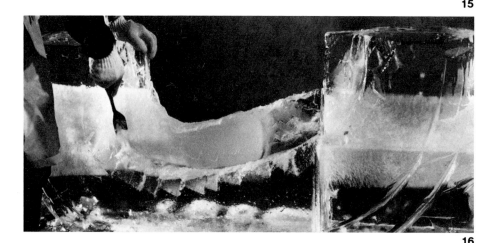

16

(3) Make the angle between the back and the fin with the angle chisel (photo 16).
(4) Make the serrated edge of the fin with the saw (photos 17 and 18).
(5) Make the scales with the flat chisel (photo 19).
(6) The back feet face both ways; carve the back part first (photos 20 and 21).

(7) Make the stomach with the angle chisel (photo 22).
(8) Make the scales with the flat chisel (photo 23).

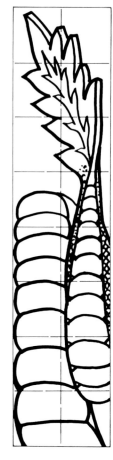

The Dragon's Tail
Ice 1 Piece

(1) Etch the outline on the ice, cut away the excess with the saw, then form the tip with the large flat chisel (photo 24).

(2) Shape the outside (photo 25).

(3) Finish the tip of the tail (photo 26).

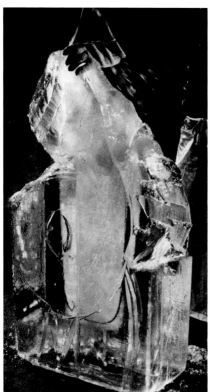

24

25

26

27

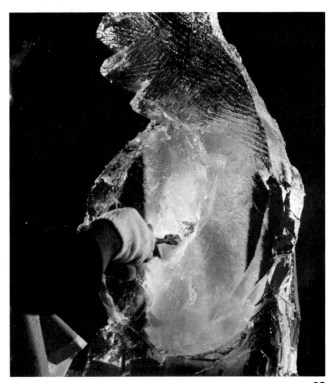

28

(4) Finish more of the outline, cutting out the angles (photo 27).

(5) Cut through the center of the tail (photo 28).

(6) Carve out the rounded stomach, using the flat chisel (photo 29).

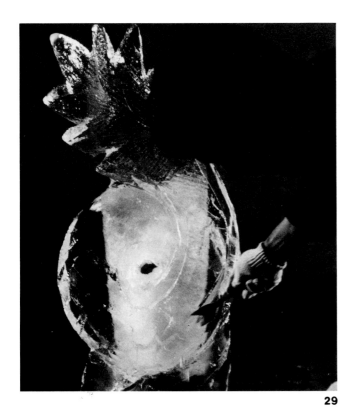

29

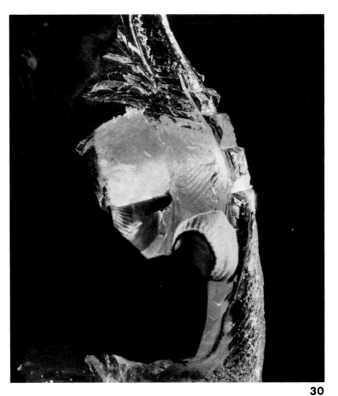

30

(7) Make the scales on the back (photos 30-32).

31

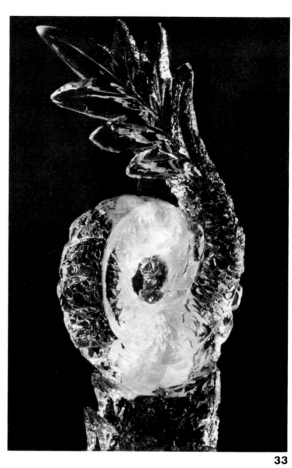

33

(8) Note the curve of the tail from photos 33 and 34.

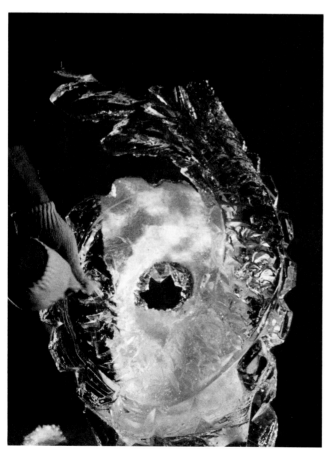

32

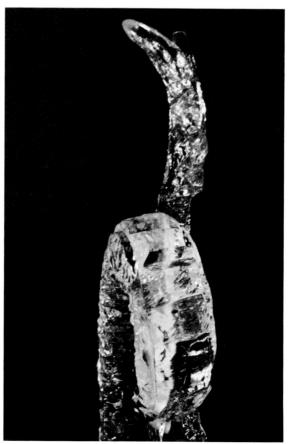

34

35

36

The Front Foot – I   Ice ½ of ¼ A Cut

(1) Etch the outline, then cut away the excess ice with the saw.
(2) Roughly shape the foot with the chisel (photos 35 and 36).
(3) Make the nails sharp (photo 37). Photo 38 is the finished foot.

37

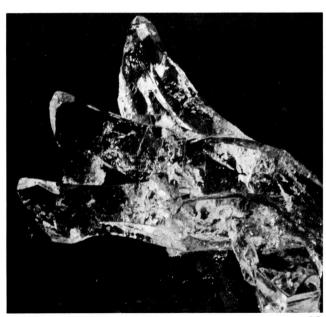

38

39

40

41

The Front Foot – II   Ice 1/2 of 1/4 A Cut

(1) Cut away excess ice with the saw, then shape the foot with the flat chisel (photos 39 and 40).
(2) Determine the thickness of the foot, then finish the toes (photos 41 and 42).
(3) Trim off the excess ice, using the edge of the chisel, as in photo 43.

42

43

The Ball and Half Ball   Ice 1/6 B Cut

(1) Both are carved as shown in photo 44.

(2) Smooth the surface (photos 45-47).

44

How to cut the balls

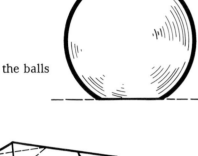

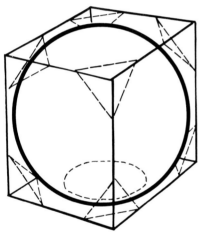

45

46

47

Stand   Ice 5, 1/2 B Cuts

(1) Place the five pieces together along the width with no gaps between the pieces (photo 48).
(2) Level the entire surface with the flat chisel, then the saw (photo 49).
(3) Cut the flutings around the edges (photo 50).

48

49

50

Assembly Of The Dragon

(1) Stand the front part of the body on the forward part of the stand (photo 51).
(2) Next, put the back part together with the front part, without gaps between the joining surfaces (photo 52).
(3) Put the head on; each joining surface must be flat (photo 53).

51

52

53

(4) Put on the tail, again without gaps (photo 54).
(5) Put the balls in front of the dragon. The front foot is 15 cm in front of the hind foot.
(6) Finish any details (photo 56).

54

55

56

4　4尾のエンゼルフィッシュ

FOUR ANGEL FISH

Ice 2, ½ B Cuts; 4, ¼ A Cuts; 2, 1/6 A Cuts

This has the combined figures of four angel fish. There are small variations in each, but all are basically the same. When the height and shape of each one are composed a bit differently, the piece has a live, dramatic feeling. Be careful that their general size is about equal, and that the delicate fins are not damaged.

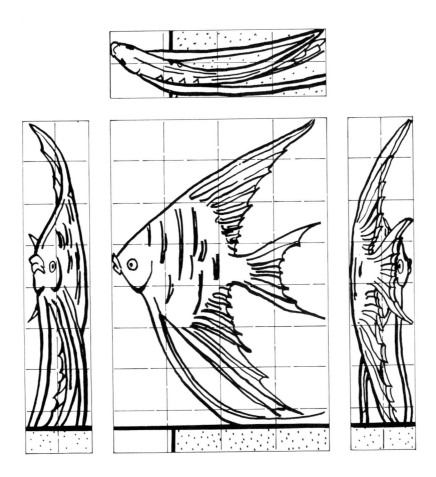

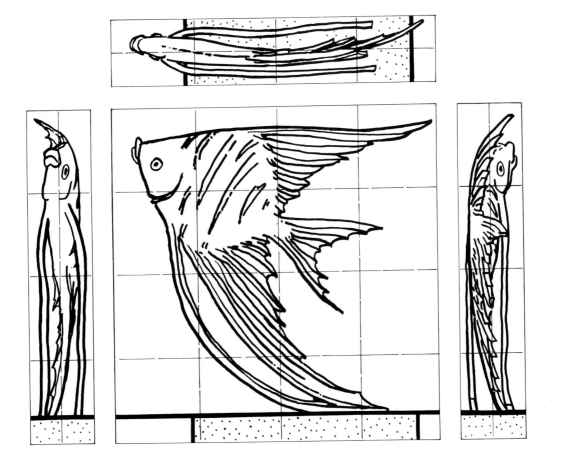

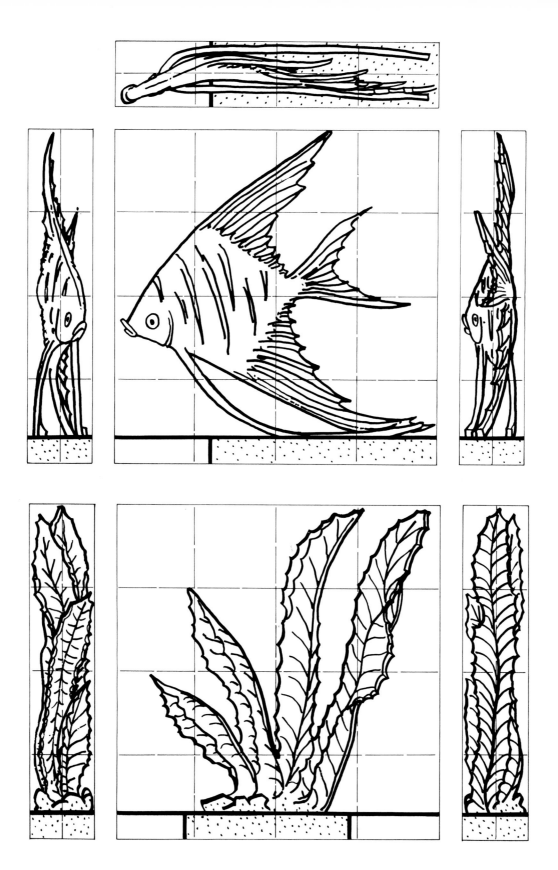

HOW TO CARVE

(1) Etch the shape of the fish, and then cut away the excess ice. Carefully check the thickness at this time (photo 1).
(2) The fins and tails arch backwards. Finish off the rough shape of the fish, fins and all (photo 2).

(3) Use the saw to shape the fish, being careful about the thickness (photo 3).
(4) Carve the mouth, gill slits, and fins with the angle chisel; carve the two long, trailing pectoral fins (photo 4).

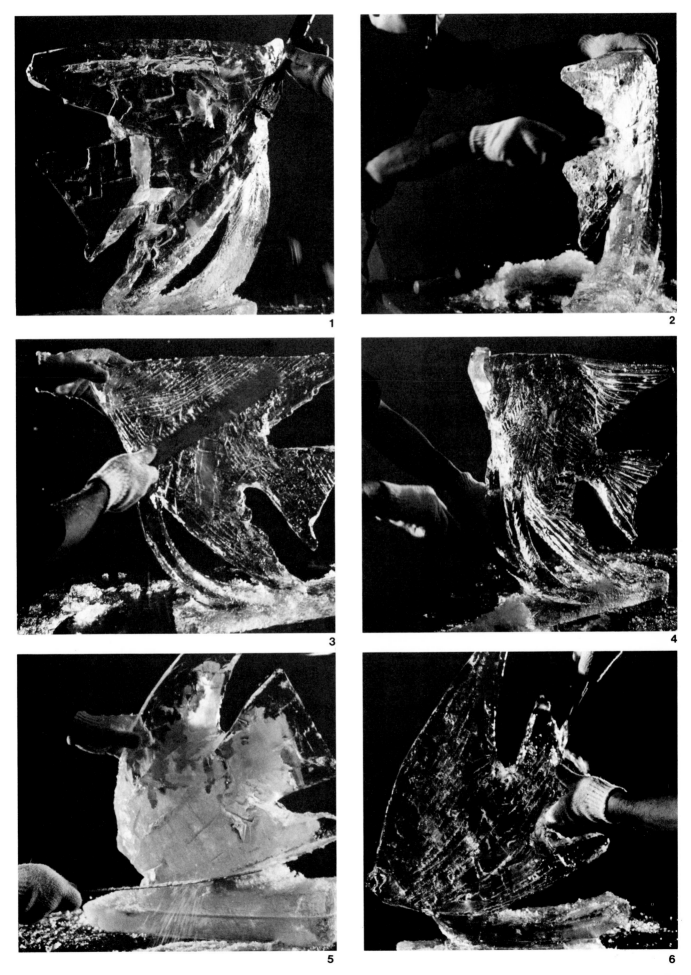

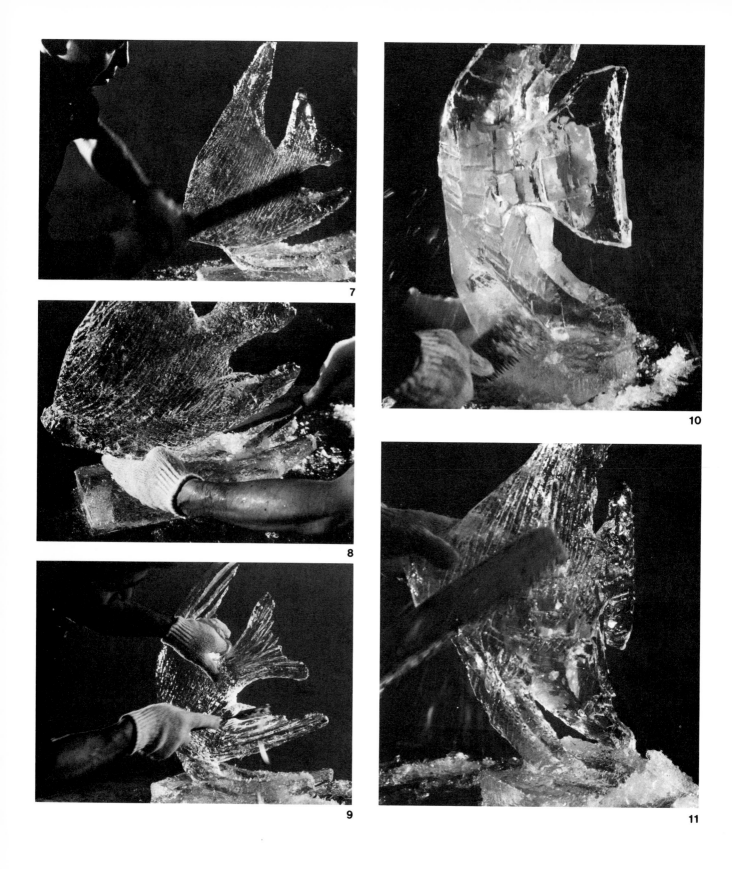

7

8

9

10

11

(5) Make the outline of the lower part of the fish, and cut away the excess ice. Trim with the flat chisel. This fish is similar to the first, but is facing downward (photo 5).

(6) Trim off the thickness and shape the tail, then shape the whole body with the saw (photos 6 and 7).

(7) Separate the pectoral fins where they touch and stand (photo 8). Make the mouth, gill slits, and fins with the angle chisel (photo 9).

(8) The other angle fish are made the same way as the first two (photo 10).

(9) Using the saw blade, shape the fish as before (photo 11), then use the chisel.

(10) Make the last fish as the rest, but in a slightly different position (photo 13).

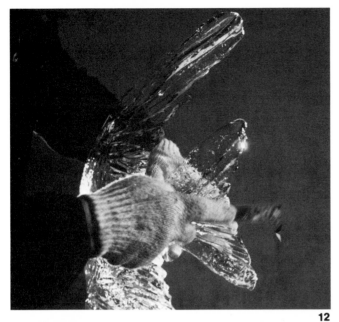

12

15

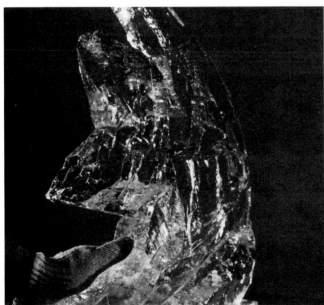

13

16

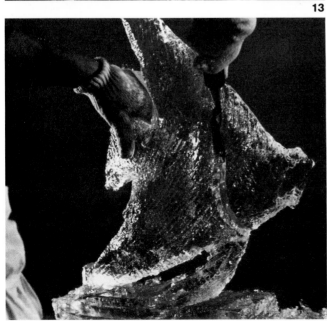

14

17

(11) Use the angle chisel to make the gill slits (photo 14).
(12) Start the strands of seaweed with the saw, then finish with the chisel (photos 15 and 16).
(13) Level the surface of the stand, cut holes into the stand the size of the stands on the fish and seaweed, and put the fish and seaweed in place (photo 17).

5 五重の塔

FIVE-STORY PAGODA

Ice 2 Pieces, 5, 3/5 Cut

There are many different five-story pagodas in Japan, which are old Shinto or Buddist temples; for example, the five-story Horyu temple in Kyoto. In this ice temple, the important thing is that each story is a bit smaller than the story below. Each story has a balustrade around the perimeter, four corners arched upwards, and a roof apparently made of tile.

OBJECTIVES

● The two main blocks are joined to make the stand, and the five other blocks are placed on them. Be sure that the joining surfaces are flat and level, or the pagoda will tilt to one side. All of the roofs and railings are carved identically, except in size, the bottom one being the largest.

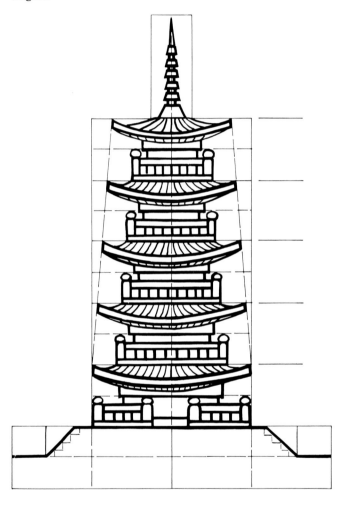

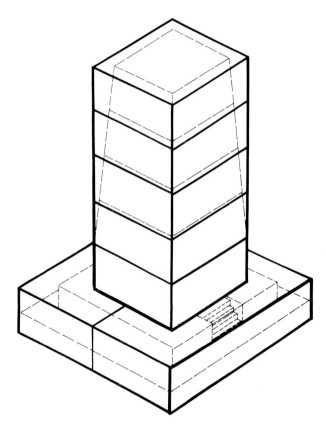

● As the blocks pile higher, it is important to keep each story in balance.

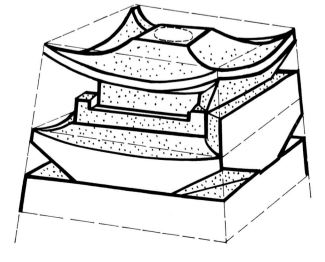

1

2

3

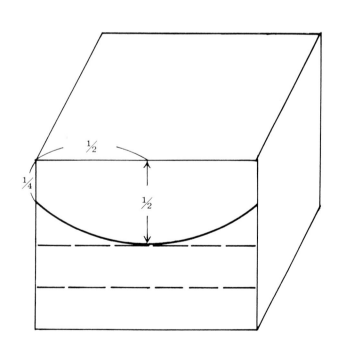

HOW TO CARVE

(1) Make the stand from the two large blocks of ice of the same thickness. Level the surface by cutting off the excess with the saw blade. Place each of the five blocks squarely on top of each other (photo 1).

(2) After positioning the five blocks, shape the sides (photo 2).

(3) Make the outline of the roof and balustrades (photo 3).

4

5

6

7

(4) Carve by starting from the top. Divide each story into four equal sections, the top of the roof line curving from the half-way point to the point 1/4 from the top. A narrow strip is carved along the lower quarter of the story (photos 4 and 5).

(5) Each story is proportionately the same (photo 6).

(6) Carve the outline of each roof (photo 7).

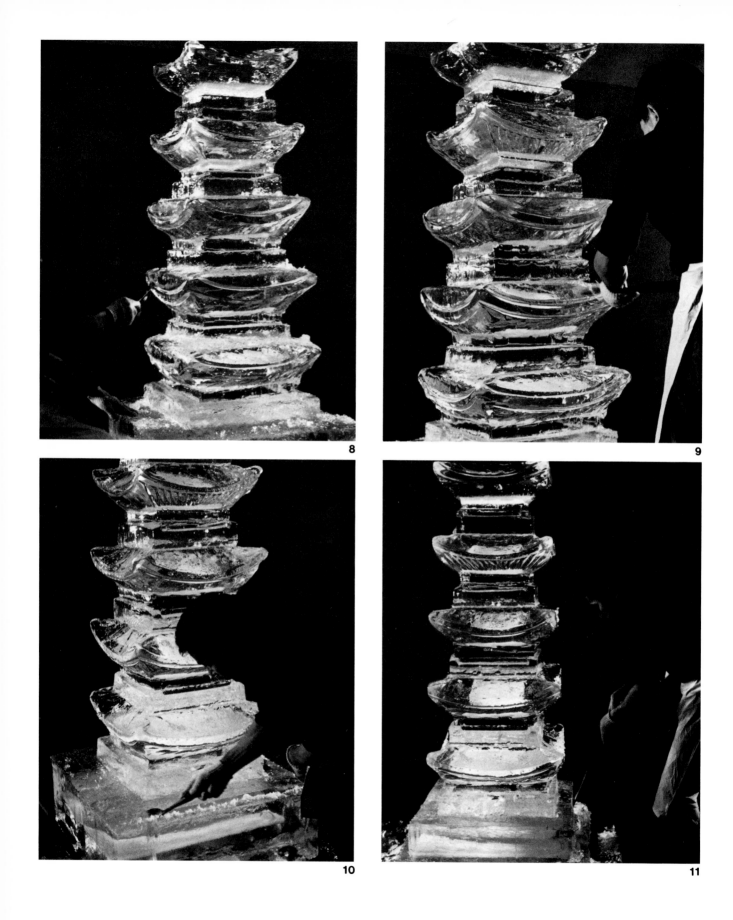

8

9

10

11

(7) The roof is arched as shown in photos 8 and 9.
(8) Make steps on each side of the base, about 5 cm wide (photos 10 and 11).

(9) Cut ridges on the bottom side of the roofs (photo 12).
(10) Using a piece of scrap ice, make the steeple that goes on the top of the fifth story (photos 13 and 14).

12

13

14

15

(11) Make the balustrade with the angle chisel, then the tile on the roof tops (photo 15).
(12) Place the steeple in the center of the top story.

ANGEL

Ice 1 Block; 2, ½ A Cuts;
2, ½ B Cuts; 4, 1/6 A Cuts; ¼ A Cut

This pretty angel on a pedestal goes well as the center piece for a more formal occasion. The head of the angel is large, but is balanced by the carefully carved arabesque base, which sets off the whole carving to advantage.

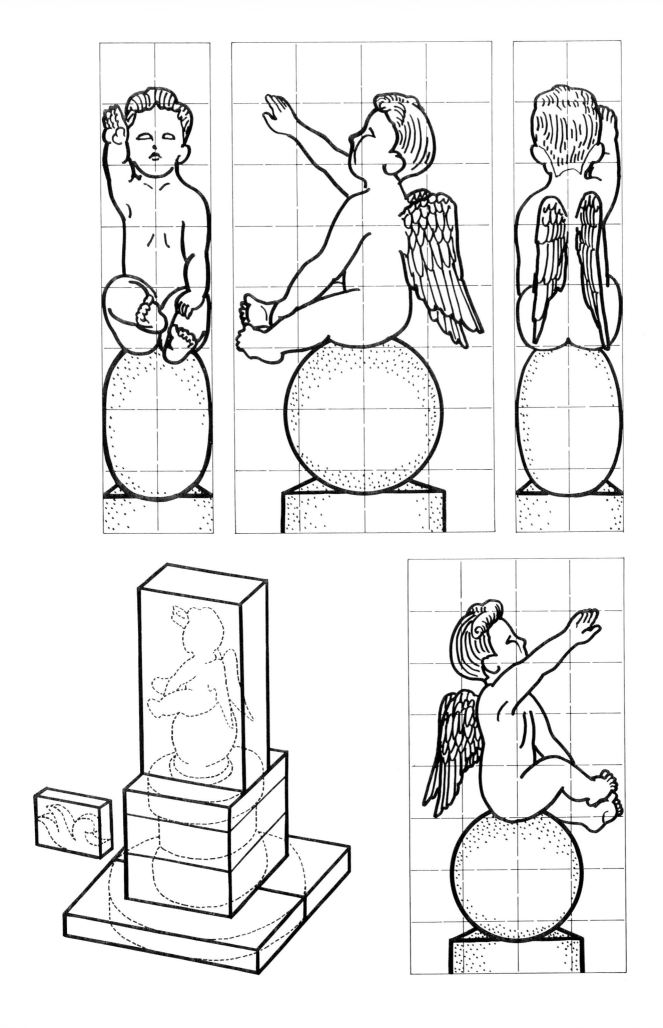

303

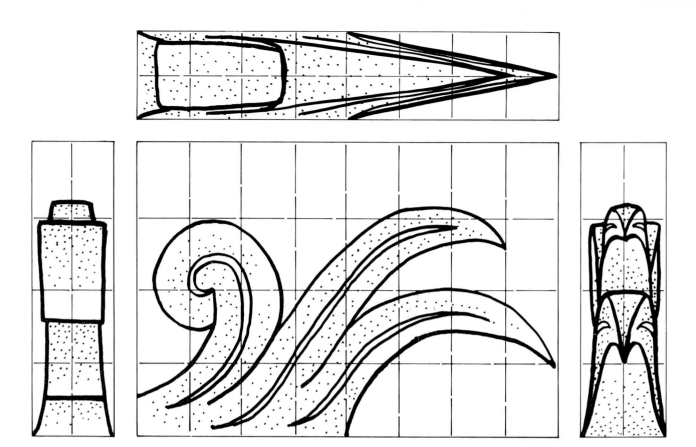

OBJECTIVES

The angel and the ball are made from the single large block, the bottom of the base is made of the two 1/2 B Cuts, the two 1/2 A Cuts, and the 1/4 A Cut. The four 1/6 A Cuts form the arabesque decorations. The joining surfaces must be flat and level, otherwise, the figure will not be stable.

HOW TO CARVE

The Stand   Ice 2, 1/2 B Cuts; 1/4 A Cut; 2, 1/2 A Cuts

(1) Make sure the surfaces of the 1/2 B Cuts are level and smooth. Using the saw, etch a rough circle on the block, then cut out the circle with the saw (photo 1).

(2) Using a piece of string, put one end in the center of the circle, and then, with the point of the chisel on the edge of the rough circle, redo the edge (photo 2).

1

2

3

6

4

7

5

8

9

10

11

12

(3) Trim off this circle with the large flat chisel (photo 3).
(4) Etch a concentric circle a bit larger than 1/2 the radius (photo 4).
(5) Cut this line about 1 cm deep with the angle chisel (photo 5).
(6) Taking the 1/2 A Cut block, level and smooth both the top and the bottom, etch a smaller circle, and cut away the excess ice (photos 6 and 7).
(7) Make a cylinder from the 1/2 A Cut with the flat side of the large chisel (photo 8).
(8) Place the cylinder on top of the larger circle, and then level the cylinder's surface with the saw (photo 9).

13

14

15

16

(9) Make a still smaller cylinder on the other 1/2 A Cut, and place this cylinder on top of the first cylinder (photo 10).
(10) Make the joint between the upper and lower cylinder smooth (photo 11).
(11) Work the surface smooth with the saw (photo 12).
(12) With the 1/4 A Cut block, make a cylinder of which the

diameter is the mean between the base (Step 1) and the middle cylinders (Steps 7 and 8), then level the top (photo 13).
(13) Divide the middle two cylinders into four equal sections horizontally. Then, with the angle chisel, encircle the cylinder at these points (photo 14).

17

18

19

20

The Arabesque Decorations   Ice 4, 1/6 A Cuts

(1) Etch the pattern, then cut out the decorations with the chisel (photo 15).
(2) Cut out the basic shape (photo 16).
(3) Cut the pattern on the sides (photo 17).
(4) Make all four pieces the same way.

The Angel and Ball   Ice 1 Block

(1) Etch the profile, then cut away the excess ice with the saw and the flat chisel (photos 18 and 19).
(2) Rough out the size of the right arm and cut away excess ice. Bring out the head, then the outline of the left arm and the front of the ball (photo 20).
(3) Cut out both wings, keeping their thickness in mind

21

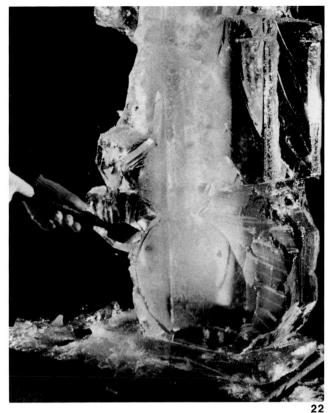

22

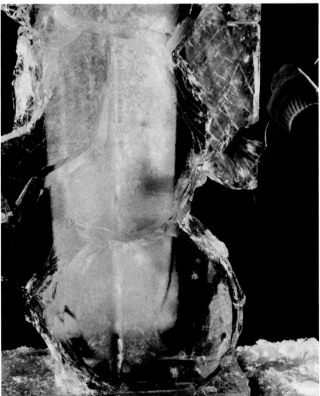

23

24

(photo 21).
(4) Next, roughly shape the ball under the angel (photo 22).
(5) Roughly shape the wings (photo 23).
(6) Shape the area from the head to the neck, from the head to the chest, and between the arms (photo 24).
(7) Make the right arm and upper half of the torso (photos 25 and 26).

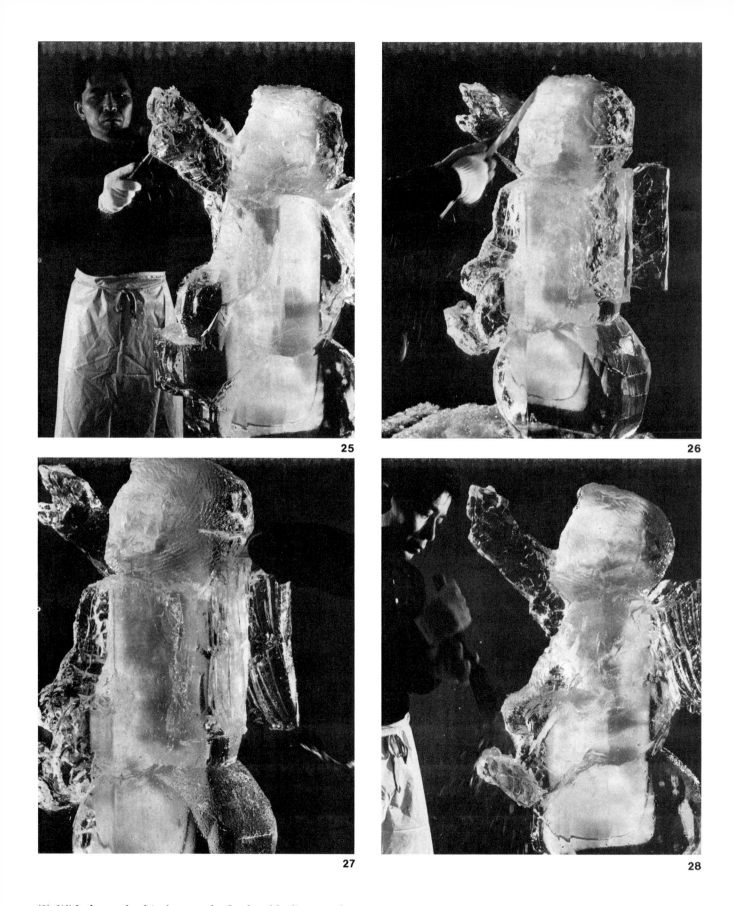

25

26

27

28

(8) With the angle chisel, carve the feather-like lines on the wings (photo 27).

(9) Do the legs next, with the right leg a bit more curved then the left. Use the saw and flat chisel (photo 28).

(10) Carve the top of the ball under the angel (photo 29).

(11) Finish both legs, and the face (photo 30).

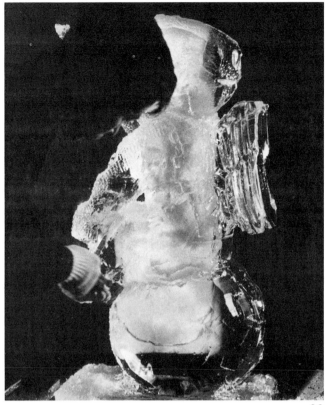

29

31

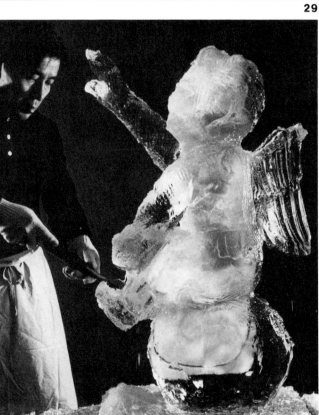

30

Assembly

Place the angel on the top of the stand, and with the angle chisel, carve the flutings around the cylinders. Place the arabesque decorations on the bottom block (photos 31 and 32).

32

7 祝と唐獅子

GROUP OF CHINESE LIONS

Ice 3 Blocks; 2, ¾ Cuts; 2, ½ B Cuts

This group is composed of mythological Chinese lions: a male and a female with a lion cub in the center. The lion cub is above the Japanese character "Shuku," meaning "congratulations," or a celebration. This piece has quite a stunning effect at banquets or at dinner parties.

OBJECTIVES

● These lions are very difficult and complicated. When done correctly, they take a lot of effort, but they can be done, just like the others.

● As this carving is quite time consuming, and the parts done first would melt before the complete group is finished, you should keep each finished piece in the freezer until it is ready for use.

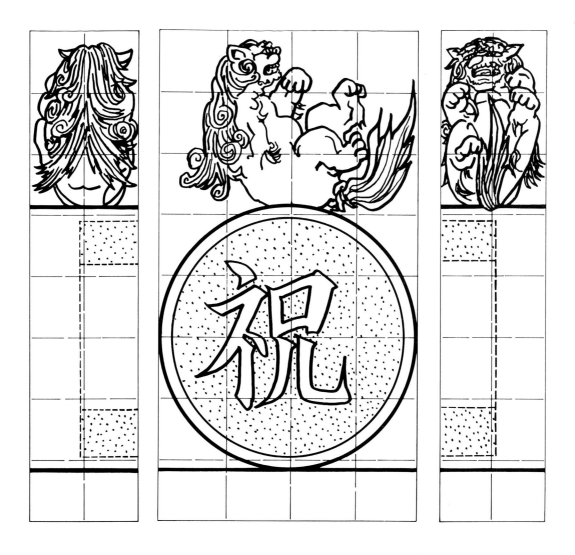

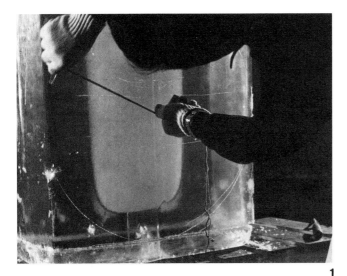

1

2

3

4

5

HOW TO CARVE

Lion Cub And Japanese Character   Ice 1 Block

(1) Etch a circle on each side of the block with a string and the chisel point, then etch a smaller concentric circle inside this circle (photo 1).

(2) Inside the small circle, etch the character "Shuku" (photo 2).

(3) Etch the figure of the lion cub, then cut away the excess

6

7

8

9

10

ice with the saw (photo 3).

(4) With the flat chisel, roughly form the lion cub (photo 4).

(5) Carve the head, forefeet, and tail (photo 5).

(6) Cut out the tail with the saw, keeping the thickness of the tail in mind. Then finish the body (photo 6).

(7) Shape the outside of the circle with first the chisel, then the saw (photo 7).

(8) Bevel the inside circle to make the character stand out in

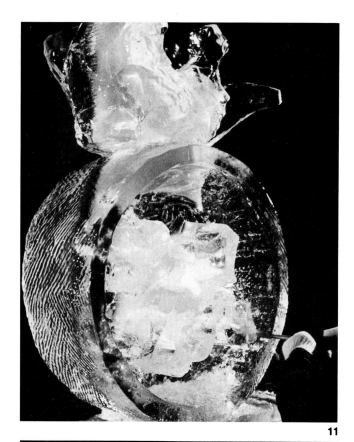

11

13

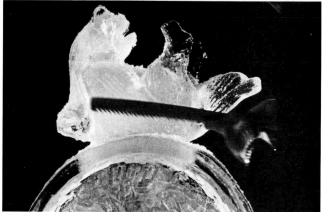

14

12

15

clear relief (photos 8 and 9).

(9) The Japanese character should appear to float in the ring (photo 10).

(10) Carefully trim the edges of the character (photo 11).

(11) Finish the lion cub's body. Etch the lines of the hair on the mane and the tail (photo 12).

(12) Finish the face and the ears (photo 13).

(13) Use the saw on the lion cub's body (photo 14). Photo 15 shows the complete unit.

  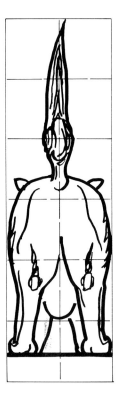

Crouching Lion   Ice 3/4 Cut

(1) Etch the outline on the ice. Cut away the excess ice, working down from the tail to the body (photo 16).

(2) Estimate the location of the ears and the curved tail, then carve them out with the angle chisel (photos 17-19).

16

17

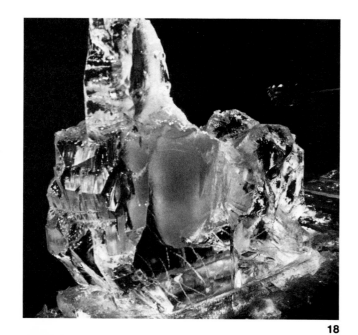

18

21

19

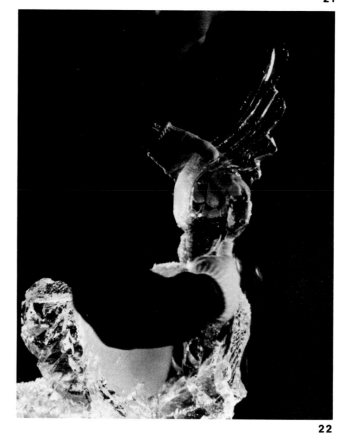

22

20

(3) Make the mouth with the saw (photo 20).
(4) Bring out the shoulder from the lower jaw to the forefeet (photo 21).
(5) Shape the entire lion. Cut the lines on the tail (photo 22).
(6) Go over the body with the saw (photo 23).

23

25

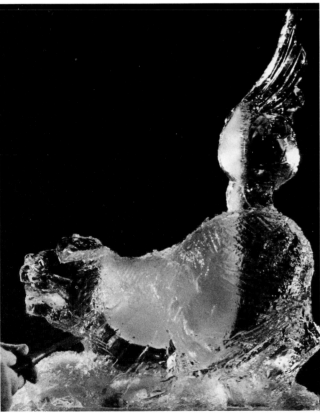

24

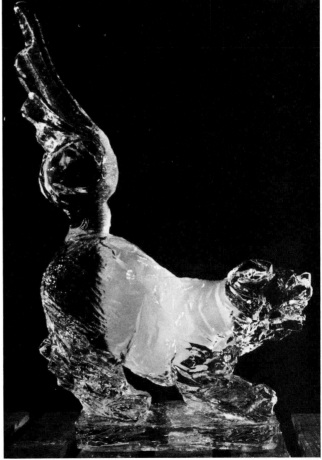

26

(7) Carve out the ears, nose, mouth, jaw, and legs with the angle chisel (photo 24).
(8) Carve the lines on the mane with the angle chisel (photos 25 and 26).

Standing Lion   Ice 3/4 Cut

(1) Etch the profile on the block of ice. Cut away the excess ice with the saw and the large flat chisel (photo 27).
(2) Curve the tail slightly (photos 28 and 29).
(3) Bring out the rough shape from tail to hips (photo 30).
(4) Carve the head, ears, and, working downwards, the lower jaw (photo 31).

(5) Roughly shape the face, then the back and the chest (photo 32).
(6) Carefully determine the thickness of the legs and the size of the lower abdomen (photo 33).
(7) Carve the tail with the saw, paying attention to the balance (photo 34).

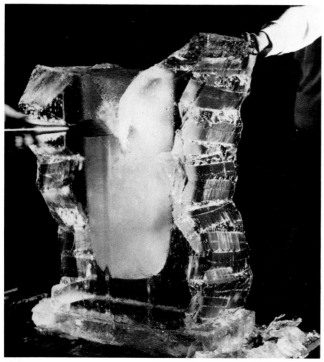

27

28

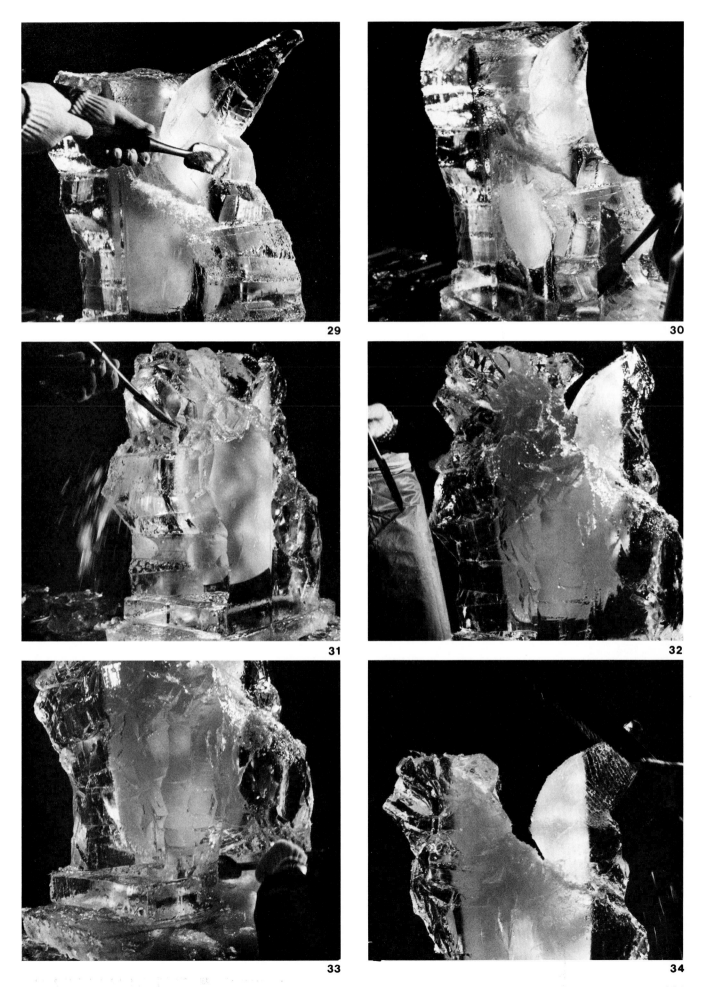

29

30

31

32

33

34

35	36
37	38

(8) Bring out the lines of the hips and the hind legs (photo 35).

(9) Separate the two front legs, making them the proper thickness in relation to the chest (photo 36).

(10) Shape the back of the neck with the saw (photo 37).

(11) Check the size of the legs and the general outline of the tail; carve the curving lines on the tail (photos 38 and 39).

39

40

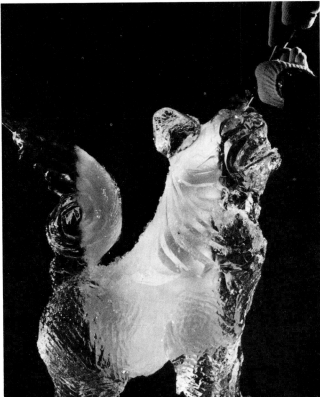

41

(12) Carve the mane with the rectangular chisel (photo 40).
(13) Finish the lion by carving the eyes, the mouth, and the ears (photos 41 and 42).

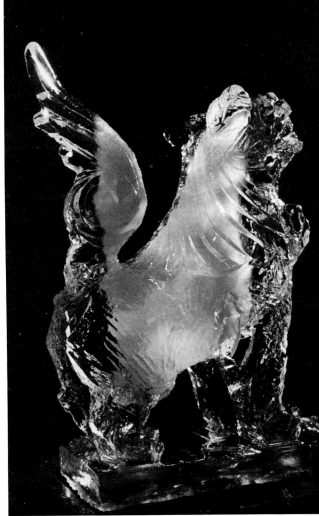

42

End Decorations   Ice 2, 1/2 B Cuts

(1) These are a combination of wave and leaf patterns. After cutting out the rough shape, cut the veins on the leaves (photos 43-45).
(2) Do the same for the second piece, then carve the curling lines (photos 46-48).

43

44

45

46

47

Center Stand   Ice 2 Blocks

- Join the two blocks of ice. Etch the outline, then cut it out along the lines (photos 49-52). Carve the decorative relief.

- The lion cub and Japanese character section will sit in the semi-circle; carve a level place for it.

48

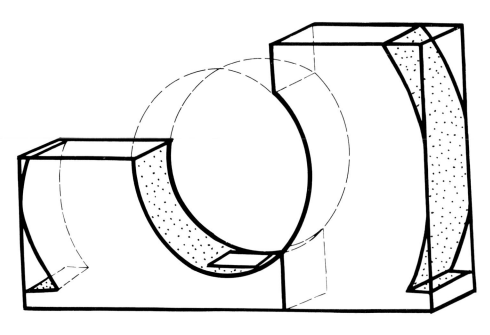

Asembly
Put the two stands together, position the end decorations in place, then place
the lion cub in the center, the crouching lion on the right, and the standing lion
on the left.

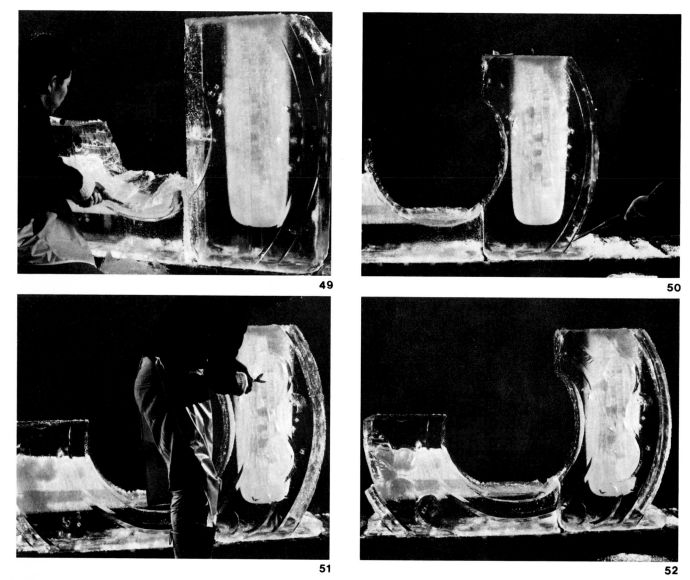

49

50

51

52

POSTSCRIPT

I think that you will be able to satisfy yourself that your work is improving step by step.

My publishing schedule started in the summer of 1972 when I was in the middle of a tour of the U.S. While looking back at this schedule, I became aware of my original hit-and-miss approach to ice carving.

This revised publication took a long three years. After two years, I quite dispaired of succeeding in the struggle. However, at last one copy was finally finished. I cut down the total number of pieces from 90 to 70. I think that these pieces can be done well if the steps in this book are followed.

It takes technique, drive, and a lot of effort to create something beautiful. At times you will make mistakes. This will, however, build up your skill step by step through experience. Failure can be regarded as a stepping stone to eventual success.

If you are completely satisfied, you cannot truly progress, nor will you fulfill yourself.

Both beginners and the more experienced have different ideas about how to carve. You must challenge yourself to solve the difficult problems. The quality of the work you will do a year from now will be different than the quality of work you can do now.

This will be due to the effort you will have put into learning the art. The history of ice carving is not long, but there is room for unlimited development in the future. I would like to see you reach as high a level as possible.

Hasegawa Hideo

Additional Books In This Series

Buffets and Receptions

The culmination of many years of writing and preparation. Chefs and restaurateurs from many countries have contributed recipes and ideas to give this book a truly international flavour.

From simple party snacks to elaborate buffets for the great occasion this comprehensive volume will provide the reader with thousands of new thoughts and ideas. Buffets and Receptions will rapidly prove to be an essential possession for every chef and caterer.

1240 pages, including 120 pages colour plates, 64 pages black and white step by step techniques and two comprehensive indexes.

Catering and Hotelkeeping

Edited by Professor John Fuller, FHCIMA. A comprehensive work of reference, invaluable to every hotelier, chef and restaurateur, and to everyone involved in any way in the hotel and catering industry. Covers every aspect of hotel and restaurant work. Contents include: kitchen records, function menus convenience foods, catering law, hotel administration, etc., etc.

2 volumes, 1190 pages, 41 chapters, nearly 300 line drawings, many full colour and black and white plates, 29 expert contributors.

Modern French Culinary Art

A new, enlarged and fully revised edition. Essentially a professional work for the chef and caterer. The recipes are clearly set out and the ingredients and quantities specified are meticulously correct. Many of the recipes are superbly illustrated in full colour. There are action photographs of kitchen preparations, special sections on gueridon service, pastry and confectionery, and a fully comprehensive index.

1,000 pages, 286 colour plates, 186 step-by-step photographs.

Fish and Shellfish

A comprehensive volume containing hundreds of international, classical and regional dishes. Designed both for the student and the professional in the modern hotel and res taurant. The excellent colour plates show exact methods of presentation for the table.

320 pages of text, 80 pages colour plates, 112 pages black and white halftones.

The New International Confectioner

Revised Metric Edition. Edited by W. J. Fance, F Inst BB. Designed for all who are interested in patisserie — the student, the amateur, the craftsman and artist alike.

908 pages, including 112 pages colour plates, 64 pages black and white photographs showing special techniques and more than 100 diagrams and drawings in the text.

The Complete Book of Meat

Edited by F. Gerrard, MBE, FInstM and F. J. Mallion. FRSH, FInstM, with 22 eminent authors, each expert in his field. New first edition. 652 pages, over 130 colour and black and white photographs, 100 drawings and diagrams.

Gueridon and Lamp Cookery

By Professor John Fuller, FHCIMA. Deals with an important aspect of restaurant service, covering sidetable service and carving and chafing dish and flambe cookery. Meets the needs of restaurant proprietors, managers and waiting staff at all levels.

162 pages, 26 black and white photographs.

For free colour brochures of any of these titles, and for information about future books, please write to:

Continental Publications
P.O. BOX 2248
PALOS VERDES, CA. 90274